De-familiarizing Readings

I0127729

EUROPEAN JOYCE STUDIES

18

General Editor: Fritz Senn
Associate Editor: Christine van Boheemen

De-familiarizing Readings

Essays from the Austin Joyce Conference

Edited by
Alan W. Friedman
and
Charles Rossman

Rodopi

Amsterdam - New York, NY 2009

The paper on which this book is printed meets the requirements of "ISO 9706:1994, Information and documentation - Paper for documents - Requirements for permanence".

Second Edition: 2010

ISBN: 978-90-420-3237-8
E-Book ISBN: 978-90-420-3238-5
©Editions Rodopi B.V., Amsterdam – New York, NY 2009
Printed in The Netherlands

For David G. Wright, eminent Joycean,
whose untimely death occurred while we were editing these papers.

CONTENTS

BIBLIOGRAPHICAL NOTE

In keeping with previous volumes in this series, the following standard abbreviations are used for parenthetical citations and other references within the texts:

CW   James Joyce, *The Critical Writings of James Joyce.* Ed. Ellsworth Mason and Richard Ellmann. New York: Viking Press, 1959.

D   James Joyce, *Dubliners: Text, Criticism and Notes.* Ed. Robert Scholes and A. Walton Litz. New York: Viking Press, 1969.

FW   James Joyce, *Finnegans Wake.* London: Faber, 1939.

JJQ James Joyce Quarterly, published by the University of Tulsa; Tulsa, Oklahoma.

Letters I, II, III   James Joyce, *Letters of James Joyce.* Volume I, ed. Stuart Gilbert. New York: Viking Press, 1957. Volumes II and III, ed. Richard Ellmann. New York: Viking Press, 1966.

P   James Joyce, *A Portrait of the Artist as a Young Man*, ed. Chester G. Anderson. New York: Viking Press, 1968.

SL   James Joyce, *Selected Letters of James Joyce.* Ed. Richard Ellmann. New York: Viking Press, 1975.

U   James Joyce, *Ulysses.* Ed. Hans Walter Gabler. New York and London: Garland, 1986. Cited by episode and line number.

INTRODUCTION

ALAN W. FRIEDMAN AND CHARLES ROSSMAN

"Joyce in Austin," the 2007 annual James Joyce Bloomsday conference, provided validation that Joyce studies (commonly known as "The Joyce Industry") remain alive and well, if somewhat differently configured than they have been in recent years. For the past quarter century or so, Joyce and other literary studies have been highly, though hardly exclusively, theoretical and ideological—deconstructive, feminist, post-colonial, psychological, political.[1] But they have lately become more solidly grounded in the "stuff" of texts, contexts, and intertexts: data and dates, food and clothing, letters and journals, literary allusions, and other quotidian desiderata. Successful inductive approaches, like the staging of a perfectly scripted legal case, must be thoroughly researched, argued with meticulous, even nit-picking, precision, and reach a persuasive conclusion that somehow seems both striking and inevitable. This legal analogy is particularly apt given the welcome outcome of the copyright abuse lawsuit against the Joyce estate approximately a month before the conference. Carol Shloss's quoting from and citing such unpublished sources as medical records and letters in *Lucia Joyce: To Dance in the Wake*, Shloss's biography of Joyce's daughter Lucia, ran afoul of the Joyce Estate. What the legal decision on the suit clearly and precisely documents is the significance of this case and its outcome that allows and encourages scholars to pursue their research and to document the results of their forensic inquiries. Although a settlement unlike a judgment technically sets no precedent, the case should positively impact all future dealings with the Joyce estate and with the issue of fair use generally. It is the stuff of future studies.

1. See, for example, Christine Froula, *Modernism's Body: Sex, Culture, and Joyce* (New York: Columbia University Press, 1996); Vicki Mahaffey, *Reauthorizing Joyce* (Cambridge: Cambridge University Press, 1988); Margot Norris, *Joyce's Web: The Social Unraveling of Modernism* (Austin: University of Texas Press, 1992); Jean-Michel Rabaté, *Joyce upon the Void: The Genesis of Doubt* (New York: St Martin's Press, 1991); Alan Roughley, *Reading Derrida Reading Joyce* (Gainesville: University Press of Florida, 1999); and Luke Thurston, *James Joyce and the Problem of Psychoanalysis* (Cambridge: Cambridge University Press, 2004).

Both Tara Prescott's "'Guttapercha things': Condoms, Desire, and Miscommunication in 'The Dead'" and Susan J. Adams' "Joyce in Blackface: Goloshes, Gollywoggs and Christy Minstrels in 'The Dead'" take Gabriel and Gretta's curious footwear as starting points for forensic explorations. Prescott traces the growing use of rubber products "after the discovery of the vulcanization process in 1843," especially the "popularization and democratization of contraceptive practices in Europe and the United States" in the late nineteenth and early twentieth century. A rich and varied vocabulary, much of which Joyce employs, developed for contraceptive products and practices, and, Prescott demonstrates, its subtle uses resonate throughout "The Dead," so that Gabriel's concern for Gretta's health, presciently well-founded given Michael Furey's "get[ting] his death in the rain," expands to include his desire to keep her from another pregnancy, another form of danger. For Adams, the fact that "the word 'goloshes' reminded Gretta of the Christy Minstrels" leads to fascinating speculation about an unlikely host of possible Joycean allusions: to minstrel shows (whose tripartite structure "The Dead" may echo), Golliwogg dolls, Teddy Bears, Jim Crow, *Uncle Tom's Cabin*, Br'er Rabbit, and Lord Nelson's green eyeshade.

In "Dating Stephen's diary: When Does *A Portrait* End?," the late David G. Wright asks this seemingly simple question concerning the dating of *Portrait*. Noting that the only year actually mentioned in the text of *Portrait* is 1829, "the time of Catholic emancipation and the tradeoffs which were allegedly made to achieve it," he argues that "Dublin 1904 / Trieste 1914," the dates and locations cited at the end, "seem to attach themselves to the text proper, much more snugly and emphatically than the analogous entries in Joyce's later books." But "Stephen generally does things later than Joyce did them," and evidence from *Ulysses* reveals that Stephen's mother's death "occurs in June 1903. ... So the year of the diary must be 1903." Wright's close scrutiny reveals much about the specifics of Stephen's life, including some inconsistencies on Joyce's part regarding the novel's chronology, while raising questions about what Stephen has been doing during the year that "has elapsed between his mother's funeral and the day of *Ulysses*."

Both Austin Briggs's "Is Bella Cohen Jewish? What's in a Name?" and Margot Norris's "Stephen Dedalus's anti-Semitic Ballad: A Sabotaged Climax in Joyce's *Ulysses*" raise questions of Jewishness within *Ulysses* that had long seemed settled. Briggs argues that, despite her name, Bella Cohen, whom Neil Davison considers "the feminine element of [Bloom's] own person—Jewish, libidinous, but yet now empowered," may not, in fact, even be Jewish. Exploring the history of Jewish and Irish name changing, Briggs finds that "Cohen is 'more usually' an Irish than a Jewish surname in Ireland." Joyce foregrounds the curious nature of Stephen Dedalus' name when, for instance, Davin in *Portrait* asks him "What with your name and your ideas - Are you Irish at all?" Bella and Bloom also bear problematic names; and, while Bella Cohen's ethnic identity may ultimately be as indeterminate as Bloom's, like Stephen they are part of that rich, multi-hued mix that comprise the Irish. Norris takes up the even more troubling issue of Stephen Dedalus' singing of "Little Harry Hughes," an anti-Semitic ballad, to Leopold Bloom at what she suggests is the climax of their meeting and perhaps of the book. Stephen's action raises several important questions: "why would Stephen, the antithesis of the anti-Semitic Garrett Deasy, do such a thing? And why would Bloom, after recovering from the impact of the song, nonetheless invite Stephen to spend the night, and perhaps become a boarder in his home?" And "How and why does the narrative strategy of 'Ithaca' prevent readers from recognizing not only the significance of the performance of the song, but also its function as a climax of the episode, and perhaps even of the novel's action?" Norris then weaves a rich tapestry of understanding of Bloom, Stephen, and their relationship out of several conversational threads they have. She traces what is said and what is implied concerning "the informed, insightful, engaged discussion and exchange that Bloom evidently craves" and Stephen's apparently uncharacteristic "brutal attack on an innocent man." Norris's thorough and tactful speculation on this conundrum—and its larger implications—leads to a surprising and powerful conclusion concerning the nature and role of anti-Semitism in *Ulysses* and beyond.

In "The Shakespearean Demiurge in Joyce's Forge," Stephen Whittaker argues that Joyce constructs elaborate expositions on the nature of creation covertly throughout his writings, but more overtly "near the centers of [both] *Ulysses* and *Finnegans Wake*." In the former work, "Stephen sketches a picture of artistic making in which the creator's creation recapitulates his ontogeny"; in the latter, the construction is a geometric figure that begins Euclid's *Elements* and also apparently depicts Anna Livia's pelvis. Both derive from Plato's "cosmic forge wherein all creation comes into being" in the *Timaeus*, with Shakespeare in the role of the demiurge who is the agent of all creation for Joyce.

And finally, Alan Shockley, in "Playing the Square Circle: Musical Form and Polyphony in the *Wake*," reminds us of some easily forgotten truths: "*Finnegans Wake* is a novel that doesn't work like a novel. . . . [I]f it has a plot, it is so simplistic [sin, fall, and resurrection] that most writers would eschew using it even to underpin a short story, much less to bolster a large novel." And it is Vico's circular view of history as well as musical form and polyphony that provide much of this unique text's richness, substance, and significance. For just as certain notes in a Bach fugue stand in for and recall other notes that might be expected, Joyce's neologisms often both displace and summon a rich complex of other words and meanings.

We hope you agree with us that this is all good stuff.

University of Texas at Austin

"GUTTAPERCHA THINGS": CONTRACEPTION, DESIRE, AND MISCOMMUNICATION IN "THE DEAD"

TARA PRESCOTT

Abstract: "Goodness me, don't you know what goloshes are? You wear them over your . . . over your boots, Gretta, isn't it?" asks Aunt Kate (*D* 181). In "The Dead," Joyce devotes a curiously large amount of space to a seemingly inconsequential pair of goloshes. The historical, medical, and cultural context of the word "gutta-percha" suggest that Gabriel and Gretta Conroy's argument over "guttapercha things" could, in fact, be a coded conversation about birth control, connecting unrequited desire, miscommunication, and a pair of rubber boots.

In her analysis of "The Sisters," Mary Lowe-Evans states that a Joyce short story "demands the breaking down of textual boundaries. Its effect on the narrator of the story and on the reader is to raise the question, 'What *else* is meant by this word?'"[1] Using this question as a starting point, I would like to consider what *else* is meant by the word "guttapercha" in "The Dead" and examine how alternate readings of the term add new insight into Gabriel and Gretta's relationship.

To an early twentieth-century reader, "gutta-percha" was synonymous with rubber, latex, and various new products that were available after the discovery of the vulcanization process in 1843. The word originates from the Malaysian term *getah percha*, meaning "gum of the percha tree."[2] This processed dark brown or black rubber material was used for a wide assortment of products, including telegraph cables, furniture, combs, picture frames, and golf balls.

Because gutta-percha was strong, it was also used for the rubber rings in intrauterine devices (IUDs) and pessaries. Softer, more elastic forms of rubber, however, were needed to make condoms. Although condoms made of animal intestines, silk, fish bladders, and other materials had been in use for hundreds of years, the introduction of pliable rubber allowed for cheaper, more reliable, and aesthetically pleasing prophylactics.

---

1. Mary Lowe-Evans, *Crimes Against Fecundity: Joyce and Population Control* (Syracuse: Syracuse University Press, 1989), p. 42. Further references will be cited parenthetically in the text.
2. *Oxford English Dictionary*, 2nd ed., s.v. "gutta-percha."

The multitude of names for rubber and rubber products reflects the different inventors who struggled to improve the material. Journalist and author Adam Hochschild gives a brief history of rubber nomenclature:

> In the late 1700s, a British scientist gave the substance its English name when he noticed it could rub out pencil marks. The Scot Charles Macintosh contributed his name to the language in 1823 when he figured out a mass-production method for . . . applying rubber to cloth to make it waterproof. Sixteen years later, the American inventor Charles Goodyear accidentally spilled sulfur into some hot rubber on his stove. He discovered that the resulting mixture did not turn stiff when cold or smelly and gooey when hot—major problems for those trying to make rubber boots or raincoats before then. But it was not until the early 1890s . . . that the worldwide rubber boom began.[3]

The "worldwide rubber boom" coincided with the writing and publication of "The Dead," which was set in 1904, completed in 1907, and published in 1914.[4] In addition to advancements in technology and transportation, the rubber boom precipitated a popularization and democratization of contraceptive practices in Europe and the United States.

Birth control choices in the late nineteenth and early twentieth century were much more varied and sophisticated than the modern reader might assume.[5] Women and men who wished to prevent pregnancies, increase the intervals between children, or limit their number of children had several options, including *coitus interruptus* (withdrawal or "incomplete" sex), mutual masturbation ("marital onanism"), the rhythm method, douches,

---

3. Adam Hochschild, *King Leopold's Ghost* (Boston: Houghton Mifflin, 1999), pp. 158-59.

4. Joyce's interest in imperialism and the rubber trade is evidenced by multiple textual references to Irishman Roger Casement. For an engaging study on Casement and the Belgians in the Congo, see Hochschild, *King Leopold's Ghost.*

5. See Janet Farrell Brodie, *Contraception and Abortion in Nineteenth-Century America* (Ithaca: Cornell University Press, 1994). Further references will be cited parenthetically in the text. Brodie notes, "In the nineteenth century there was no established language for what we today call 'birth control.' Before Margaret Sanger succeeded in the early twentieth century in introducing that forceful and assertive label, birth control was referred to in more labored language as 'the prevention of conception,' 'the limitation of offspring,' 'the prevention of pregnancy,' 'the anti-conception art,' 'preventatives,' 'regulating reproduction,' 'limitation of family,' 'regulators,' 'checks,' and 'the laws regulating and controlling the female system'" (5). For the purposes of this essay, "birth control" and "contraception" are used interchangeably to refer to behavior methods (withdrawal, rhythm method) and devices (condoms, diaphragms) used to prevent conception.

sponges, diaphragms ("womb veils"), pessaries, abortion, and, most commonly, rubber condoms.[6]

Initially, rubber condoms were associated mainly with prostitution and "used more as a prophylactic against infection than as a contraceptive,"[7] a practice that gradually changed. Although the mid-century Comstock Laws, which made the transmission of indecent materials through the mail illegal, severely hindered public access to contraceptive knowledge and materials in the United States, the amount and variety of prophylactics available was large, and "rubber contraceptives were ubiquitous by 1900" (Bullough 111). One study of the sale of contraceptives in England found that "after 1890 contraceptives were widely available, mostly made of rubber" (Bullough 110). As Mary Lowe-Evans indicates, "Between 1876 and 1931, birth control became legitimate, respectable, and, to some extent, a civic duty" (3). Malthusian fears of overpopulation, combined with population-related tragedies such as the Irish Famine in the 1840s, pushed many couples to delay marriage (as often happened in Ireland) and consider having smaller families (as happened particularly in France, Britain, and the U.S.). People living on the Continent had access to official contraceptive clinics and, in some countries, were even able to purchase condoms sold in machines (Bullough 109).

But Catholic Ireland had much tighter restrictions on contraceptive material than did Europe and America. The Church outlawed contraception, and the sale and advertisement of contraceptive devices and medications was forbidden. Wealthy Irish people, however, often traveled to England and the Continent, where contraceptives were prevalent. Depending on social class, access to urban areas, and need, the Irish would have known about and had limited access to many of the contraceptive methods used abroad. Joyce owned several books about the Catholic Church's stance on "non-procreative sexuality," as well as several texts "expressing a variety of views on the subject of birth control, including Shaw's *Getting Married* and a Fabian tract, 'The Decline in the Birth-Rate'" (Lowe-Evans 25).

6. In a letter to Burt Green Wilder, David Humphreys Storer wrote, "'Whatever may be said to the contrary by superficial observers, there can be no doubt that intercourse, unless *complete*, is prejudicial to the health of both parties" (quoted in Brodie, *Contraception*, 271). The habit of describing *coitus interruptus* as "incomplete" informs Bloom's reaction to the advertising slogan, "What is home without Plumtree's potted meat? Incomplete" (*U* 8.742-43).

7. Vern L. Bullough, "A Brief Note on Rubber Technology and Contraception: The Diaphragm and the Condom," *Technology and Culture* 22 (January 1981): pp. 104-11. Further references will be cited parenthetically in the text. *Ulysses* allows this association to resonate by referring to condoms in the Nighttown section. Bloom also shows concern about "some chap with a dose burning him" and, in relation to Blazes Boylan, thinks, "No, no. I don't believe it. He wouldn't surely?" (*U* 8.6).

As societies grappled with the propriety of discussing these products, they developed various slang and shorthand terms. Just as Americans today refer to condoms by the material they are composed of ("rubbers"), the Victorians and early Edwardians also used shorthand terms for their prophylactics, mainly based on the material. Throughout his works, Joyce utilizes many slang terms for condoms, including "Macintosh" (*U* 15.1560-65), "prophylactic" (*U* 17.241-42), "French letter" (*U* 13.877), "rubber preservatives" (*U* 15.1571, 17.1804), and "immaculate contraceptives" (*FW* 45.14).

Joyce's deployment of the word "macintosh*"* in *Ulysses* shows the same utilization of synecdoche and metonymy that links rubber boots and contraception in "The Dead." The word "macintosh" is derived from the name of the inventor of the rubber material from which the coats were made. According to historian Janet Brodie, "the Englishman Charles MacKintosh discovered waterproof garments that could be created by sandwiching between two fabrics a layer of rubber dissolved in cool naphtha" (209). Mackintosh's name became synonymous with the material he discovered, and, by extension, the items created with that material.

Joyce encountered at least one rich source for exploring the connection between rubber protective wear and sexuality: Sigmund Freud. In *The Interpretation of Dreams* Freud describes the analysis of a dream by a young man:

> *He dreamt that he was putting on his winter overcoat again: this was terrible.* The occasion for the dream is apparently the sudden advent of cold weather . . . what could be terrible about wearing a thick or heavy coat in cold weather? Unfortunately for the innocency of this dream, the first association, under analysis, yields the recollection that yesterday a lady had confidentially confessed to him that her last child owed its existence to the splitting of a condom. . . . The condom is a "pullover" (*Ueberzieher* = literally pullover) for it is pulled over something: and *Ueberzieher* is the German term for a light overcoat. An experience like that related by the lady would indeed be "terrible" for an unmarried man.[8]

In this case, Freud demonstrates how the young man man's unconscious has substituted an overcoat for a far more threatening object, a condom. Through a similar process of substitution, Bloom sees the terrible "man in the macintosh" multiple times during the day while he is thinking about his wife having sex with another man, and Gabriel blushes profusely over a pair of

8. Sigmund Freud, *The Interpretation of Dreams*, trans. A.A. Brill (New York: Modern Library, 1994), pp. 89-90.

goloshes while unsuccessfully flirting with a housemaid. Condoms, like overshoes (goloshes) and overcoats (mackintoshes), are rubber items that must be pulled over a part of the body. To push the analogy one step further, one could argue that the use of the "pullover" item actually overtakes the wearer in some fashion. Like Freud, Joyce sees beyond the benign surface of images to evoke the multiple resonances and associations contained within the words.

In her groundbreaking history of contraception in America, Janet Brodie notes that "most nineteenth- and even early twentieth-century novelists could not openly address contraception and abortion. Readers may wonder yet have to remain ignorant about how Dreiser's Sister Carrie avoided pregnancy" (1). Joyce, however, is a notorious exception, and his unabashed pursuit of describing and including the totality of human life, including sex and contraception, occurs in all of his works, which also demonstrate a persistent interest in adultery, paternity, fertility, pregnancy, birth, and sterility. The thorough examinations of these themes in *Ulysses* and *Finnegans Wake* began as initial forays in *Dubliners*.

As "The Dead" begins, Gabriel Conroy arrives at his aunts' Usher's Island house wearing a pair of goloshes that will shortly become a key conversation piece. After he enters the house, he begins "scraping the snow from his goloshes" and "scraping his feet vigorously" to clean off the "light fringe of snow" (*D* 177). Although this action by itself is unremarkable, the vigorous scraping calls the reader's attention to Gabriel's fastidiousness (to avoid dragging wet shoes into the home), his trendy footwear (goloshes were popular at the turn of the century), and the snow itself (the first time that snow appears in a story which famously ends with snowfall).

As Gabriel takes off his cloak and prepares for the party, he makes conversation with Lily, the Miss Morkans' beleaguered servant. Lily's youth and beauty attract Gabriel despite his position as an older, married man and paternal figure who has known her since her childhood. Lily and Gabriel trade meaningless remarks about the weather and school before Gabriel accidentally stumbles into an emotional minefield by suggesting that Lily will be marrying soon. With "great bitterness" Lily responds, "The men that is now is only all palaver and what they can get out of you" (*D* 178). Immediately afterward, "Gabriel coloured as if he felt he had made a mistake and, without looking at her, kicked off his goloshes and flicked actively with his muffler at his patent-leather shoes" (*D* 178). It is curious that, when Gabriel realizes that he is one of those "palaver" men who sexually hungers for Lily, his first action is to kick off his goloshes. Clearly, Gabriel does not feel "as if" he has made a mistake—he knows he has. He automatically responds to Lily's "bitter and sudden retort" (*D* 179) by blushing, chucking his boots aside, and becoming engrossed in his shoes, revealing his guilt and a desperate need to change the subject of conversation.

If this scene were the only place where the goloshes made their appearance, the reader would likely dismiss them as a distraction. The goloshes soon become the focal point of conversation, however, suggesting that they play a prominent role in the story. In fact, in light of the rest of "The Dead," Gabriel's encounter with Lily establishes a connection between forbidden or unrequited desire, miscommunication, and a seemingly innocuous pair of rubber boots.

Thrusting a coin into Lily's hands, Gabriel scurries off to escape the awkward encounter and join the rest of the party. Eagerly awaiting Gabriel are his two doting aunts, Julia and Kate. The narrator notes that Aunt Julia has a "flaccid" face but stands "erect" (*D* 179). The adjectives, while innocent, introduce a subtle phallic vocabulary that prepares for the coded conversation that follows. As the aunts and the Conroys discuss Gabriel's having secured a hotel room for the night to protect his wife from going home in the cold, Gretta interrupts:

> —Don't mind him, Aunt Kate, she said. He's really an awful bother, what with green shades for Tom's eyes at night and making him do the dumb-bells, and forcing Eva to eat the stirabout. The poor child! And she simply hates the sight of it! . . . O, but you'll never guess what he makes me wear now! (*D* 180)

In these sentences, Gretta moves seamlessly from Gabriel's over-protection of their children to his over-zealous attention to her attire, although her examples are hardly out of the ordinary. Concern for reading in low light, promoting a child's physical activity, and forcing a child to eat a food he or she dislikes are all well within the realm of normal parenting. Gabriel's attention in these examples hardly justifies Gretta's labeling him "an awful bother." As Gretta laughs, Gabriel's "admiring and happy eyes" wander "from her dress to her face and hair" (*D* 180). The conversation has started lightly: he is admiring her form and appearance much as he will again later when she is on the staircase, and again when she is in bed. But the tone of the conversation quickly changes as Gretta launches into her next story of Gabriel's solicitude. "You'll never guess what he has me wear now!" she taunts, indicating both how unexpected Gabriel's request is and hinting at possible scandal:

> —Goloshes! said Mrs Conroy. That's the latest. Whenever it's wet underfoot I must put on my goloshes. To-night even he wanted me to put them on, but I wouldn't. The next thing he'll buy me will be a diving suit.
> Gabriel laughed nervously and patted his tie reassuringly while Aunt Kate nearly doubled herself, so heartily did she enjoy the joke.

The smile soon faded from Aunt Julia's face and her mirthless eyes were directed towards her nephew's face. (*D* 180)

In this exchange, Gretta reveals her husband's odd fascination with "the latest" fad, his emphasis that she "must" participate in it, and her own refusal. She ends the story with an exaggerated prediction, implying that Gabriel will move from merely covering her feet in rubber to encasing her entire body in it. Gabriel's response to this allegation, nervous laughter, could suggest that Gretta is making a fool out of him in front of his aunts and he is too polite to stop it. His nervousness, however, could also be due to the fact that the discussion is not merely about wearing goloshes, but rather that Gretta is consciously or unconsciously referring to another disagreement that the couple has had in private: over whether or not to engage in birth control. Just as Mr. Browne assumes a low Dublin accent to tell a bawdy tale in mixed company, the coded goloshes conversation allows Gretta to air sexual or marital grievances against Gabriel publicly. In fact, when Aunt Kate doubles over in laughter, it could be because she is aware of a different "joke" than the exaggeration of the diving suit. Less sophisticated than her sister, Aunt Julia nonetheless realizes that Gretta is challenging Gabriel about a serious issue, which is why her smile fades and her "mirthless eyes" fix on Gabriel.

After a pause, Aunt Julia then asks, "And what are goloshes, Gabriel?" (*D* 181). Curiously, she does not address the question to Gretta, who was telling the story and who used the word "goloshes." By doing so, she attempts to divert the conversation away from Gretta, who is humiliating her husband, to Gabriel, giving him control of the story. But Aunt Kate intercedes:

> —Goloshes, Julia! exclaimed her sister. Goodness me, don't you know what goloshes are? You wear them over your . . . over your boots, Gretta, isn't it?
> —Yes, said Mrs Conroy. Guttapercha things. We both have a pair now. Gabriel says everyone wears them on the continent.
> —O, on the continent, murmured Aunt Julia, nodding her head slowly. (*D* 181)

In this exchange, Joyce shows Aunt Kate hesitating noticeably before revealing where on the body one wears goloshes. Given that the conversation was about walking in the snow, getting wet, and keeping Gretta safe from cold, it is unlikely that Aunt Kate has forgotten that goloshes are worn on the feet. So why does Joyce break Aunt Kate's thought at "You wear them over your . . ."? The pause could indicate that Aunt Kate is unsophisticated enough that she would not feel certain about goloshes. This would not, however, reveal anything about her character that is not adequately shown in other parts of the story. Instead, the hesitation suggests that the conversation is straying into uncomfortable territory or, perhaps, that the parties are discussing more than footwear. Because Aunt Kate understood "the joke" in the previous interchange, she may be covering for Gabriel and Gretta here, continuing the conversation and leading Aunt Julia to believe it is *only* about goloshes. She could be sharing a joke with the Conroys while the more conventional Julia remains naively and sweetly unaware.

After Gretta clarifies "goloshes" by calling them "guttapercha things" that her husband claims are all the rage "on the continent," Aunt Julia nods her head slowly in understanding, either because she realizes that fashions originate in Europe before they reach Ireland or because she realizes that prophylactics, which were difficult to acquire in Ireland, were freely available abroad.

According to Brodie, "the control of reproduction known by some was secret information, spread sometimes directly but often by innuendo—a cautious and reticent dissemination of sought-after but almost illicit knowledge" (2). The use of innuendo, and Gabriel's increasing anger over the course of the conversation, provides evidence that more is at stake here than mere overshoes:

> Gabriel knitted his brows and said, as if he were slightly angered:
> —It's nothing very wonderful but Gretta thinks it very funny because she says the word reminds her of Christy Minstrels.
> —But tell me, Gabriel, said Aunt Kate, with brisk tact. Of course you've seen about the room, Gretta was saying. (*D* 181)

Just as he reacted "as if" he had made a mistake with Lily in the first scene, here Gabriel reacts "as if" he is angry. The narrator's qualification of Gabriel's behavior may indicate that Gabriel is trying his hardest to maintain a façade but, despite himself, reveals deeper feelings. The conversation shows Gabriel's shift from lovingly admiring his wife to verbally insulting her in the way she has insulted him, forcing the reader to ask what has provoked him and what the conversation reveals about his relationship with Gretta.

Several reasons exist for Gabriel's anger. At the literal level, he is angry because his wife is mocking his concern for her. Gabriel may also pride himself on his worldly, sophisticated, even taboo knowledge of the most current contraceptive methods practiced on the Continent, and instead of being scandalized by this knowledge, the women laugh at him. According to Norman E. Himes, "contraceptive knowledge always has been, and still is to some extent, the possession essentially of the upper, more privileged classes."[9] Margaret Sanger describes an incident where Catholic women begged her to find out what secret "Yankee" and Protestant women had for avoiding pregnancy.[10] Gabriel, who believes he has special knowledge, reminds himself that "their grade of culture differed from his" (*D* 179). The socialization and democratization of birth control had, however, changed it from being a privilege of the elite on the Continent to something available to the middle and working classes as well. Given Gabriel's fear of being misunderstood and his constant references to his own exalted status, it would be reasonable to read this scene as a glimpse into his insecurity regarding sexual relations with his wife. He takes her health seriously, has done the delicate research of discovering how to protect her, has even traveled to the places where the items necessary for protection are available, and not only does she refuse to take part, but she also mocks him for it.

By shifting the conversation to Gretta, Gabriel makes her the new object of ridicule. Gretta's visual and phonetic association of goloshes with Christy Minstrels indicates an embarrassing lack of sophistication and betrays Gabriel's fear that she is, in fact, "country cute" (*D* 187). Edwin T. Christy's minstrel shows featured performers in blackface known as "gollies" or "golliwogs." Since "the word" reminds Gretta of the minstrels, she may be confusing "goloshes" with "golly shoes," "gollies," or "golliwogs." Goloshes were also typically made of dark brown or black guttapercha, so Gretta may make the connection based on color. Before Gabriel can explain the nature of Gretta's word association, Aunt Kate expertly performs damage control and changes the subject. The fact that she uses "brisk tact" for the situation could be due to her fear that a marital quarrel is about to erupt, or that a highly improper coded conversation about contraception may be getting out of hand.

As Brodie notes, "gutta-percha products could be as innocent as goloshes or a coded term for condoms."[11] Other Joyce texts tie "gutta-percha" to male anatomy, and specifically to anatomy that cannot procreate. In the "Lotus Eaters" chapter of *Ulysses*, Bloom sees carriage horses and muses, "Gelded too: a stump of black guttapercha wagging limp between their haunches" (*U* 5.217-18). Here, "guttapercha" comes to Bloom's mind because the black color and texture of the flaccid horse penises match the color and texture of rubber.

If one reads "guttapercha things" as merely goloshes, this scene depicts Gabriel as greatly concerned for his wife's welfare. Although Gretta mocks and publicly humiliates him for being overly protective, one could argue that

9. Norman E. Himes, *Medical History of Contraception* (New York: Schocken Books, 1970), p. 210.
10. Margaret Sanger, *My Fight for Birth Control* (Elmsford, NY: Maxwell Reprint, 1931), pp. 49-53.
11. Janet Brodie, interview by author, 7 December 2006.

Gabriel has admirable reasons for worrying about his wife's feet. First of all, there is a precedent for Gretta's frailty, as "Gretta caught a dreadful cold" after the previous year's party (*D* 180). Catching cold could easily lead to pneumonia, and the threat of death-by-cold is very real by the end of the story, when Gretta reveals that her childhood love Michael Furey died after standing in cold rain waiting for her (*D* 223).

At face value, the goloshes scene provides insight into the dynamic between Gabriel and Gretta. When pushed further, however, the scene may also provide vital details about their sexual relationship. Gabriel's need to protect Gretta is all-consuming and valiant, but she seems to view his doing so as a burden. The motif of protection begins with the goloshes and extends until the final scene, when Gabriel longs to "defend her against something and then to be alone with her" (*D* 213). His desire to protect her, like his desire to have sex with her, is thwarted by Gretta's misunderstanding of his intentions, her own detachment, and the still living memory of Michael Furey. Particularly in the bedroom, the memory of death extinguishes any possibility of intimacy between Gretta and Gabriel, as it has done for Molly and Bloom.

A similar conflation of death, sexual imagery, and protection appears in the advertising handbills and newspapers that Joyce would have seen abroad. This typical "ABORTISEMENT" (*FW* 181.33) for galoshes depicts this connection (see Figure 1).

Figure 1. Advertisement for goloshes. John Wyse Jackson
and Bernard McGinley, *James Joyce's Dubliners* (New
York: St. Martin's Press, 1993), p. 162.

Advertisements for contraception also capitalized on protection and fear of
physical harm. "In both the pamphlets and the longer works the single most
important rationale offered for family limitation was preservation of a wife's
health," notes Brodie (182). Joyce was certainly aware of the toll pregnancies
took on women; his own mother endured seventeen pregnancies and died
before her forty-sixth birthday (Lowe-Evans 26). Childbirth was likely to be
prolonged—as it is for Mina Purefoy in *Ulysses*—dangerous, or fatal. The

Conroys have two children; however, there is no information about what Gretta's pregnancies were like, how many miscarriages or stillbirths she may have had, or how long Gabriel and Gretta have been married. The Conroy's children figure in the story only in Gretta's allusion to them as anecdotal evidence for her husband's over-protection.

The "guttapercha things" could be protection against water or semen, illness or pregnancy: Gabriel has good reason to believe any of these may lead to death. Regardless of whether or not Gabriel's fears are justified, if Gretta loved him, she would indulge his small request, or at least refrain from mocking him about it in public. At a basic level, the goloshes discussion reveals Gabriel's intense concern for his wife and her lack of reciprocal concern, something Gabriel fails to realize until the final scene.

An obvious problem with a "contraceptive reading" of the goloshes scene is that it is the woman who refuses to wear the "gutta-percha things," not the man. The fact that the item in question is on Gretta's body might invite the idea that the "guttapercha things" are a substitute for diaphragms, which were available, made out of gutta-percha, and worn by women at the time. The preposition "on" does not exclude that option, as diaphragms are worn on the cervix. More likely, the emphasis on Gretta's decision shows that family planning had to be agreed upon by both partners and Gretta has refused to give her consent, perhaps because of a conflict in religious beliefs between her and Gabriel. If Gretta is a devout Catholic, birth control would be out of the question. Gabriel's national allegiance, however, and therefore his religion, is assailed throughout "The Dead." Miss Ivors accuses him of being a "West Briton" (*D* 188), and his British or Protestant leanings could indicate an openness to contraception that Connacht-born Gretta would not share. By refusing to use "guttapercha things," Gretta is taking a stand and refusing Gabriel, possibly rejecting him sexually as well as emotionally.

Gretta and Gabriel's sexual and emotional disconnection may be a precursor to the relationship of Molly and Bloom. Molly references the couple (and, interestingly, either Gretta's dress or goloshes), when she asks Bloom, "What had Gretta Conroy on?" (*U* 4.522). The similarity of the two couples and their two sterile bedrooms reinforces the point that, in many ways, "The Dead" is a study of loneliness, alienation, miscommunication, and the usurpation of old traditions and values by the new. The story seems deceptively straightforward until the final scene, which forces the reader to revisit all the clues of the evening that have led Gabriel to this one last passionate attempt to connect with his wife just as she is as remote from him as she can possibly be. The amount of space given to a seemingly inconsequential discussion about shoes forces the reader to consider other possibilities, and Joyce's sustained interest in contraception, paired with the historical association of "guttapercha" with rubber and condoms, leads to the conclusion that, as is often true for Joyce, the correct interpretation is not *either* goloshes *or* condoms, but both. Gretta misconstrues Gabriel's love for her as an annoyance; Gabriel misunderstands Gretta's emotions, and these feelings, though evident early in the story, do not become apparent to Gabriel until it is too late.

Claremont Graduate University, California

JOYCE IN BLACKFACE: GOLOSHES, GOLLYWOGGS AND CHRISTY MINSTRELS IN "THE DEAD"

SUSAN J. ADAMS

Abstract: Why does the word "goloshes" appear eight times in *The Dead*? Jackson and McGinley propose that Gretta connects "goloshes" with the Christy Minstrels because she hears the word as "golly shoes." Golly shoes connect with the Golliwogg, a children's storybook character based on a black rag doll in minstrel attire. Joyce was well acquainted with minstrel shows: repeated allusions to this form of entertainment occur in *The Dead* and the historical antecedents of minstrelsy in Irish/African music inform the story. In addition, the structure of the story is broken into three main segments, echoing the three parts of a classic minstrel show.

Introduction

It has long puzzled me why in "The Dead" the word "goloshes" reminded Gretta of the Christy Minstrels.[1] A few Joyceans over the years have nipped at this allusion, but none has tackled it head-on. Of course, like everything in Joyce, snow is not simply snow and goloshes are not simply Guttapercha rain shoes. As Joseph S. O'Leary comments about "The Dead," it is an example of "Joyce's characteristic supersaturated, exhaustive motival textures, which are so rich that almost any association they suggest will turn out to have been thought of already by the author, who has deftly integrated it in his web."[2]

This paper explores the "web" more widely and suggests that several other keys in the story help to explain why this fascinating tidbit is included—with the word "galoshes" used no less than eight times. The main argument of this paper is that the three parts of "The Dead" mimic the three parts of the traditional American minstrel show.

John Wyse Jackson and Bernard McGinley, in their edition of *Dubliners*, suggest that Gretta associates goloshes with the Christy Minstrels because she hears the word as "golly shoes."[3] The allusion to the Christy Minstrels is

---

1. I am grateful to David Wright (University of Auckland, deceased January 2008) for conversations on this topic, and dedicate this paper to his memory.

2. Joseph S. O'Leary, "Enclosed Spaces in 'The Dead,'" http://josephsoleary. typepad.com/my_weblog/2005/06/enclosed_spaces.html.

3. John Wyse Jackson and Bernard McGinley, ed., *James Joyce's Dubliners: An Illustrated Edition With Annotations* (London: St. Martin's Press, 1993), p. 163.

important because Joyce wants the reader to make the connection with the minstrel show, a subject with which Joyce was familiar, according to Bowen.[4] Looking at the Golliwogg historically and the links to the minstrel tradition opens a portal into reading "The Dead" whereby some of the other odd references in the story start to make sense.

A Golliwogg's Cakewalk[5]

The Golliwogg[6] was a fictional doll drawn by the British artist Florence K. Upton in annual children's stories created for the Christmas market beginning in 1895. Upton based the Golliwogg character on a black rag doll she had had as a child growing up in America; the doll had a jet-black face, wild wooly hair, a large smile, bright eyes and formal minstrel attire (see Figure 1). Such rag dolls were one of the most popular toys for girls in the 1800s, alongside Dutch dolls—also known as "penny dolls" or "stick dolls."[7]

Margot Norris includes the following note in her recent critical edition of *Dubliners*: "The word 'goloshes' may remind Gretta of 'christy minstrels' by way of the word 'golliwog'—another racial stereotype in the form of a grotesque, animated Negro doll." Margot Norris, ed., *Dubliners: Authoritative Text, Contexts, Criticism* (New York: Norton, 2006), p. 157n2. Finally, Robert Spoo mentions the golliwogg connection in "Uncanny Returns in 'The Dead,'" in *Joyce: The Return of the Repressed*, ed. Susan Stanford Friedman (Ithaca: Cornell University Press, 1993), pp. 89-113.

4. Zack Bowen, "Joyce, Minstrels, and Mimes," *JJQ* 39.4 (Summer 2002): pp. 813-19.

5. This section title is borrowed from the musical piece by Claude Debussy, "A Golliwogg's Cakewalk," one movement of his *Children's Corner Suite*, 1906.

6. Note the spelling of this word ending with two "g"s, which later morphed into "golliwog" and evolved into the slang "wog." Unfortunately, while the original Golliwogg exhibited valorous traits, the later Golliwog character in Enid Blyton's *Noddy* stories exhibited nasty traits and may have led to the pejorative use of the term and the banning of the dolls. For further information about the historical view of the golliwog, see "The Golliwog Caricature," Jim Crow Museum of Racist Memorabilia, Ferris State University, http://www.ferris.edu/jimcrow/golliwog/.

7. Rag dolls, mainly in animal shapes, date back to Roman times; humanized rag dolls appear to have sprung up much later. See "Soft Toys," Collecter C@fe, http://www.collectorcafe.com/article.asp?article=790.

Figure 1. From *The Adventures of Two
Dutch Dolls and a "Golliwog"* by
Florence K. Upton and Bertha Upton,
1895.

The first of the annual verse-and-picture books was entitled *The
Adventures of Two Dutch Dolls and a Golliwogg* for the Christmas market in
1895, and up until 1909 another twelve books were published in the series.
Published in both the US and the UK, they had their widest success in
Britain. After the introduction of the "Teddy Bear" into the children's toy
market in 1902-3,[8] the Upton books portrayed the Golliwogg as "Teddy's
best friend" and made it a heroic, loveable figure.

Gabriel-as-Golliwogg is a tempting image, particularly when we look at
Upton's 1895 cover illustration of the Golliwogg between two penny dolls;
Gabriel's self-description as a "penny boy" for his two aunts comes to mind.

8. In 1902, after a hunting trip, President Theodore Roosevelt refused to shoot a
tied-up bear and was cartooned for being such a good sport. The cartoon drew the
immediate attention of a Brooklyn, NY shopkeeper (Morris Michtom), who displayed
two toy bears in his store window. Michtom recognized the immediate popularity of
the new toy and requested and received permission from Roosevelt to call them
"Teddy's Bears." At the same time as it was born in the United States, the Teddy Bear
was also born in Germany. The Steiff Company of Giengen produced its first jointed
stuffed bears during the same 1902-1903 period.

I have no evidence that Joyce was aware of the Upton books or the Golliwogg character, but given the timing of publication of the series and the fact that golliwogg dolls (circa 1900) from both Italy and the UK are still traded by collectors, it is probably a safe assumption. The fact that the Golliwogg became the Teddy Bear's best friend in the series also may help explain why Freddy Malins is referred to as "Teddy." Likewise, the Golliwogg/rag doll allusion also links to the seemingly idle reference to Lily's carrying a rag doll as a child, as well as to Molly Ivors' derisive reference to Gabriel's writing for a "rag": the *Daily Express*.

The Golliwogg allusion is an important linchpin to many other interesting aspects of the story, including Freddy's comment about the Negro chieftain singing in the Gaiety pantomime. The more subtle connections emerge when one compares the structure of the traditional minstrel show to the structure of "The Dead" and its characters, and the larger context of Anglo-Irish relations to US (and European) racial relations at the turn of the twentieth century.

The Structure of the Minstrel Show[9]

The traditional minstrel show was a uniquely American theatrical form that was highly popular from about 1840 to 1895 and largely disappeared from professional venues by about 1910. It derived musically from Irish dance with African syncopation and ritually from "rough music" celebrations, including the English "shivaree," the Italian "charivari," and the Black West Indian "John Canoe."[10] The revelers (usually from the working classes) went door to door performing a traditional skit involving the same stock characters: a king, an evil one, a doctor, a hero, and several supporting roles. The hero is slain by the evil one and then, at the king's request, is resurrected by the doctor. The satanic figure is usually portrayed by an actor in blackface (or by a black actor in whiteface in the case of Africa and the Black West Indies), representing, broadly, "the Other." As the son of a Cork man, Joyce would probably have appreciated the use of burnt cork as the standard makeup of blackface.

The minstrel show gained popularity in America among Irish performers and African Americans in particular. In the American class hierarchy of the mid-1800s, African and Irish descendents were both at the bottom rung; in

9. Much of this section was guided by Frank W. Sweet, *A History of the Minstrel Show* (Palm Coast, FL: Backintyme Press, 2000) and "Minstrel Show," Wikipedia: The Free Encyclopedia, http://en.wikipedia.org/wiki/Minstrel_show.

10. The name derives from revelers shouting out "John Canoe," thought to derive from the Ewe language for shaman, "zhan-ki-nu." See Dale Cockrell, *Demons of Disorder: Early Blackface Minstrels and their World* (Cambridge: Cambridge University Press, 1997), p. 41.

this shared adversity, the two groups' musical traditions coalesced, with entertainment derived from flute, banjo, tambourine and bones (like castanets).

As the minstrel show became a more formal type of entertainment, Thomas Rice introduced one of the two stock comedy figures of the era, drawing on universal trickster folklore about the country bumpkin whose luck and nascent cleverness help rescue him from disaster. This character in Yoruba culture is a crow called "Jim." Likewise, George Dixon, another early minstrel, created the second stock character, named "Zip Coon," as a foil to "Jumping Jim Crow," in the image of a pretentious city slicker, plotting devious strategies and getting caught in his own trap. Once these stock figures emerged, E.P. Christy then polished the form and managed the Christy Minstrels, the most famous troupe of its kind. These shows blended African syncopated rhythms with catchy Celtic melody, borrowing from the work of Thomas Moore (Irish) and Stephen Foster (American) for the various entertainments in the show. In fact, Foster had his first "Ethiopian Melodies" published under E.P. Christy's name.[11]

The Christy Minstrels established the basic three-part structure of the minstrel show in the 1840s. Part One, called "The Opening," was sometimes presaged by the actors' parading to the theater and ascending to the stage doing a dance called the "walk around" or "walkabout." Upon the direction of the Interlocutor (a sort of host or emcee), the cast arranged themselves in a semicircle and sat down. The entertainment consisted of a series of ballads, comic songs and instrumental numbers, with jokes interspersed. The repartee was usually between Mr. Tambo and Mr. Bones, or between them and Mr. Interlocutor, who was always trying to restore decorum. Lyrical songs tended to focus on nostalgic longing for the simpler time in the rural South, endorsing the myth of happy slaves. One minstrel, usually a tenor, came to specialize in this part.

Part Two of the show was "The Olio," a series of short theatrical acts. These were often parodies of legitimate theater, skits and orations, with Shakespeare the usual target of parody, particularly *Hamlet*. The highlight of this part was the "stump speech," a long oration delivered by a dimwitted character trying to speak eloquently, delivering bitter social messages without offending the audience. This segment of the show sometimes ended with "parade skits," a series of outlandish characters interacting with a gatekeeper.

11. "Minstrels and Musicals: Hard Times," *Lift Every Voice: Music in American Life*, University of Virginia Library, http://www/lib.virginia.edu/small/exhibits/music/minstrels.html. For a more complete history of Foster's songs, see Ken Emerson, *DOO-DAH!: Stephen Foster and the Rise of American Popular Culture* (New York: Da Capo Press, 2001).

27

Part Three, "The Afterpiece," rounded out the production. This part of the show evolved later and often involved a skit set on an idyllic plantation with an Uncle Tom character. This segment deteriorated into slapstick humor over time and often included a dandy character, a northern urban black man trying to live above his station by mimicking white upper class speech and dress (often the Zip Coon character).

David Wright highlights the use of dotted lines in "The Dead" to demarcate the three parts of the story.[12] I am struck by the parallels between the three parts of the minstrel show, outlined above, and the three parts of "The Dead." Specifically, "The Dead" is broken into two main parts and an afterpiece, each separated by the ellipses noted by Wright. The two main parts of the "show" occur in the Morkans' house; the third occurs as the party leaves the house and moves onward.

Representing the Opening, the various characters in "The Dead" arrive at the Morkan house, with Gabriel, as the strutting and fretting Interlocutor, posed between Tambo (Aunt Julia) and Bones (Aunt Kate, who picks a bone at dinner). Browne, a rather dapper fellow, echoes a Zip Coon type of slickness. Freddy is a comically awkward character in the manner of a jumping Jim Crow, with his bronchitic laugh and unsteady movements. Ironically, in the minstrel shows, the Jim Crow character is a buffoon who often speaks the truth; Freddy may represent this character when he comments innocently about the Negro chieftain's grand voice in the panto. And Molly Ivors has "a crow to pluck" with Gabriel.

As the story moves to Part II, an Olio performance structure emerges as Mary Jane performs her academy piece, while Gabriel glances up at a Shakespeare scene. The dancing ensues, and then Aunt Julia performs her party piece. This second part is capped off by Gabriel's falsely sentimental and affected speech. In this part of the story, Molly Ivors resembles an Uncle Tom character, defending the virtue of her nationality. While the tenor's song would normally appear at this part in the minstrel show, Bartell D'Arcy's song is delayed (due to his laryngitis) until Part III; instead, the dinner guests talk *about* famous Irish tenors.

In Part III, demarcated again by ellipses, the Joyce "minstrel show" continues into the Afterpiece, including the slapstick of Gabriel's pacing in a circle as Johnny the horse. Browne appears again as the Zip Coon dandy, wearing his long green overcoat with mock astrakhan cuffs/collar and fur cap. Sentimental pieces from Uncle Tom's Cabin were often performed during the third part of the minstrel show, an action paralleled by Gabriel's final surrender westward, imaginatively joining the sentimental journey that Molly and Gretta urged him to take toward the Celtic Twilight.

12. David G. Wright, "Dots Mark the Spot: Textual Gaps in *Dubliners*," *JJQ* 41.1/2 (Fall 2003/Winter 2004): pp. 151-59.

"De Wild Goose-Nation" and Br'er Rabbit: Animal Allusions

"De Wild Goose-Nation," an American song composed by Dan Emmett, a famous blackface minstrel performer, was broadly popular in both Europe and America.[13] This song may link to the goose dinner in *The Dead* and to Gabriel's pent-up frustration, which causes him to want to carve a flock of geese.[14]

Another animal allusion may explain why Molly Ivors is described as staring at Gabriel with her rabbit's eyes. In the context of this discussion it recalls the character of Br'er Rabbit in the Uncle Remus stories by Joel Chandler Harris that began appearing in 1879. The character of Uncle Remus was "essentially, like the idyllic vision of minstrelsy, a figment of white fantasy---Harris saw Remus as having 'nothing but pleasant memories of the discipline of slavery.'"[15] Molly Ivors, an apologist for traditional Irish culture as the path to Irish independence, perhaps recalls the sentimentalist view of American slaves as enjoying their peaceful plantation life. In the American incarnation of these stories, which can be traced back again to trickster figures in Africa, the Br'er Rabbit character represents the black slave who uses his wits to overcome circumstances and to enact revenge on his adversaries, the white slave owners.[16] Perhaps this notion vindicates Molly Ivors' using her "Irishness" to challenge British imperialism.

13. William J. Mahar, *Behind the Burnt Cork Mask: Early Blackface Minstrelsy and Antebellum American Popular Culture* (Chicago: University of Illinois Press, 1999), p. 373n37. The song was dedicated to "Jim Crow" Rice.

14. Historically the Wild Geese was a name given to Irish soldiers who served in European armies after being exiled from Ireland. The Fenians transported to Western Australia adopted the phrase for themselves during their voyage on board the *Hougoumont*, even publishing a shipboard newspaper entitled *The Wild Goose.*

15. Nick Tosches, *Where Dead Voices Gather* (New York: Little, Brown, 2001), pp. 39-40. Coincidentally, it was from the Uncle Remus stories that Ezra Pound drew the nickname "Possum" for T.S. Eliot and the nicknames "Tar Baby" and "Br'er Rabbit" for himself.

16. Though not always successful, the efforts of Br'er Rabbit made him a folk hero, but the character employs extreme measures to deal with extreme circumstances. Secondly, Br'er Fox is called to mind in "The Dead" when Gabriel recalls the vest that his mother made him with little fox heads on it; curiously, one of the Uncle Remus Tales (no. 4) is titled "How Mr. Rabbit Was Too Sharp for Mr. Fox." Does Molly trump Gabriel with her arguments? See Joel Chandler Harris, *The Complete Tales of Uncle Remus* (1955; reprint, Boston: Houghton Mifflin, 1983), pp. 11-13. Yet another unusual link here is that the Br'er Rabbit stories were written down by Robert Roosevelt, uncle of Theodore Roosevelt, the original "Teddy Bear." Robert Roosevelt first published the story of Br'er Rabbit and the Tar Baby in *Harper's Weekly;* in nineteenth-century Southern black speech, a "baby" referred to a child's doll. A tar baby is therefore like a golliwogg.

A final coincidence is that Beatrix Potter, the author of the "Peter Rabbit" stories, brought them out in late 1902 with Frederick Warne & Co., whose claim to fame hitherto had been their purchase of the British rights to *Uncle Tom's Cabin*. The Peter Rabbit books were published on the crest of the popularity of Upton's Golliwogg books and Grant Richards' publication of *The Story of Little Black Sambo* in 1899. Potter, for different reasons than Joyce, had difficulties getting her books published by Richards and went to Warne by default, where she became hugely successful.[17]

Uncle Tom and Little Eva

Joyce leaves no details to chance. Gabriel's children, Tom and Eva, are mentioned by name and provide another layer of symbolic significance to the story. In the American novel *Uncle Tom's Cabin*, Harriett Beecher Stowe depicts Uncle Tom, the compliant slave, acting as nursemaid to Eva St. Clare, a little white girl who dies (apparently of consumption, like Michael Furey), but wills that her father free all his slaves upon her death. A song written in 1853, "The Death of Little Eva and Uncle Tom" by Chas L. Bennison and Isaac N. Bonney, and dedicated to Harriet Beecher Stowe, includes the following lyrics: *"Near the arbor in the garden stands the weeping willow, drooping o'er the mossy grave of Eva St. Clare."*[18] Gretta's mention of Gabriel's forcing Eva to eat the "stirabout" or oatmeal porridge recalls the "walkabout" of the minstrel show.[19]

The story mentions offhandedly that Tom uses a green eyeshade to protect his eyes. The historic figure who famously used a green eyeshade was Lord Horatio Nelson, whose pillar stood (until 1966) in front of the General Post Office in Dublin, another reminder of British imperialism along with the Wellington monument in Phoenix Park (mentioned twice in the story) and the statue of Uncle Billy (William of Orange). Nelson had a special eyeshade built into his naval hat by Locks the Hatter to protect his good (left) eye from the sun. The only portrait of Nelson with this special attachment was by

17. Linda Lear, *Beatrix Potter: A Life in Nature* (London: Allen Lane, 2007), 144-55. Coincidentally, Potter called her publisher (and later fiancé) "Johnny Crow" (175).

18. Chas L. Bennison and Isaac N. Bonney, "The Death of Little Eva & Uncle Tom," *Uncle Tom's Cabin* and American Culture: A Multi-Media Archive, The Institute for Advanced Technology in the Humanities, University of Virginia, http://www.iath.virginia.edu/utc/songs/evatomdie.html.

19. While most versions of "The Dead" show Gabriel's daughter's name as Eva, the recent Norris edition of *Dubliners* (taking the text from the Gabler 1993 edition) uses the name "Lottie" (Norris, *Dubliners* 156), which was perhaps taken from *Aunt Lottie's Stories for the Young* (Boston: G.W. Cottrell, 1859), another children's book of the mid/late nineteenth century.

William Devis (see Figure 2).[20] The military connection is reinforced when Gabriel recalls the picture of his brother Constantine as a lad in his "man o' war suit."

Figure 2. Portrait by Arthur William Devis
of Vice-Admiral Horatio Nelson, National
Maritime Museum, London.

Conclusion

This essay considers possible connections between the political and social context of America and Britain in the mid-late 1800s and how they may have influenced Joyce's thinking about the Irish question and his own quest for identity in a modern Europe. While the extent to which Joyce might have been familiar with either the slave literature such as *Uncle Tom's Cabin* or the children's literature at the turn of the century is uncertain, his knowledge

20. While it is uncertain whether Joyce knew of this special device on Nelson's hat, he did have a copy of *The Story of Lady Hamilton* by Esther Hallam Moorehouse Meynell (London: T.N. Foulis, 1911) in his Trieste library, though it included no pictures of Nelson. See Michael Patrick Gillespie, *James Joyce's Trieste Library: A Catalogue of Materials at the Harry Ransom Center, The University of Texas at Austin* (Austin: Harry Ransom Center, 1986), p. 164.

of the world would surely have included at least passing familiarity with these genres.

Only one book in Joyce's Triestine library collection explores racial issues deeply and directly: Sydney Olivier's *White Capital and Coloured Labour*.[21] Thus, while we cannot presume the connections as fact, the above-noted mention of odd details in "The Dead" offers another delectable layer of exploration. While images as simple as a rag doll or Tom's green eye shade seem random when first reading "The Dead," deeper examination suggests that they resonate with symbols of more complex sociological and political layers in the story.

University of the South Pacific, Fiji

21. See Gillespie, *James Joyce's Trieste Library*, p. 179.

DATING STEPHEN'S DIARY: WHEN DOES *A PORTRAIT OF THE ARTIST* END?

DAVID G. WRIGHT

Abstract: Although only a single historical date --1829 -- is specified in *A Portrait of the Artist as a Young Man*, the crucial year during which Stephen writes his diary entries can be established with certainty as 1903. Based on that date, major episodes in the novel can also be dated. The Christmas dinner scene, for example, takes place on December 25, 1891, and all of Chapter III occurs during just a few days in December 1898. Precise knowledge of the dates in *A Portrait* helps us to recognize the level of control that Stephen gains over his experience by the end of the novel, and to understand the backdrop to Stephen's reappearance in *Ulysses*.

At first glance, *A Portrait of the Artist as a Young Man* seems to cover a period of almost twenty years in the life of Stephen Dedalus. But few dates are actually specified in the novel. The novel's single "historical" reference is to the year 1829, the time of Catholic emancipation and the tradeoffs which were allegedly made to achieve it (*P* 38). That is the only year named within the text, and the reference might chiefly serve to remind us that the years in which the novel's present action unfolds remain, by contrast, undeclared. The only other years specified anywhere in the book make their appearance immediately after the text proper has ended, ostensibly marking places and dates associated with the composition of the novel: "Dublin 1904 / Trieste 1914" (*P* 253). Similar annotations, of course, will appear at the end of *Ulysses* and of *Finnegans Wake*. Among these three examples, however, only the entry in *A Portrait* is arranged with the years in question on two separate lines. Thus, the years specified in *A Portrait* run down the page instead of appearing side by side, as if they were continuing through into future time the sequence of lines of text in the novel itself. They also seem to attach themselves to the text proper, much more snugly and emphatically than the analogous entries in Joyce's later books because what immediately precedes them is something congruent with the idea of marking out temporal sequences: the final entry in Stephen's diary, explicitly dated 27 April, but with the year unnamed in the text. That omission seems all the stranger, and all the more noticeable, given that two other particular years are specified just after the diary apparently comes to an end.

The annotation "Dublin 1904 / Trieste 1914" could apply to Stephen as well as to Joyce. The close juxtaposition of the annotation and the diary, indeed, seems to point us in this direction. If we make such a connection, we are all the more likely to consider the question of the year in which Stephen writes his diary: the annotation poses the question of available years quite pointedly. We know from *Ulysses*, whose factual matrix accords with data in *A Portrait* at all measurable points, that after *A Portrait* ends Stephen goes to Paris, and that he is subsequently summoned back to Dublin because of his mother's impending death, which occurs in June 1903 (she is buried on 26 June 1903, to be exact [*U* 17.952]). Nearly a year later, on 16 June 1904, Stephen seems ill at ease in Dublin and lacking in direction and purpose. He shows a restless tendency to sever connections with his existing residence, place of work, and so on. "Dublin 1904 / Trieste 1914" might then hint at a possible future trajectory for him, one which *Ulysses* does nothing to rule out. In other words, Stephen could easily leave Dublin again later in 1904, and he could as well fetch up in Trieste as anywhere else: he might still be there ten years later. But that possibility remains in the realm of speculation since, after *Ulysses*, Stephen drops out of sight altogether.

What we can establish with certainty, nevertheless, is the year when Stephen writes his diary entries, which span the thirty-nine-day period from 20 March to 27 April. Stephen's mother appears in a late entry for 26 April, "putting [Stephen's] new secondhand clothes in order" for his forthcoming trip to the Continent (*P* 252). Since we know from *Ulysses* that she dies in June 1903, we can be sure that the diary predates that time, so it cannot be set in March and April 1904, even though the annotation "Dublin 1904" immediately after the diary ends might at first tempt us to suppose that it is. But it also becomes clear from the evidence in *Ulysses* that Stephen's stay in Paris, cut short by the summons to his mother's deathbed, will be brief, covering probably about five weeks. He brings back from Paris to Dublin five issues of a weekly magazine, and that surely suggests the duration of his stay: in fact, this information may well appear in the novel precisely in order to supply such a clue. It seems likely that Stephen sets off for Paris on the day immediately after he writes the final diary entry: that is, on 28 April, or exactly forty days after the diary begins. (The "fortieth day" has several apt connotations in the Bible, the Easter season, and the calculation of the solar year.) Why else should the diary end at that precise point? Stephen will then be recalled to Dublin about five weeks later, in the first week of June. So the year of the diary must be 1903. No other possibility fits the facts: March and April 1902 would be much too early, and by March and April 1904 Stephen's mother will be dead and unable to help him with his clothes or anything else.

The date of Stephen's trip turns out to be one of numerous instances where Joyce changed the details of his own life before grafting them onto Stephen, since his own first departure for Paris had taken place not in April

1903 but in December 1902. In fact, Stephen generally does things later than Joyce did them, and it is an intriguing implication of the concealed but precise dating of *A Portrait* that it so consistently demonstrates this pattern of delay. Joyce's own recall to his mother's deathbed in Dublin happened on Easter 1903, about halfway through the period of time covered by Stephen's diary: in 1903, Good Friday fell on 10 April. It may have seemed to Joyce poignant or ironic, though this would be purely a "private" reference, that the date of his own sad return to Dublin should cut across the time when Stephen is still enthusiastically planning his initial departure from Dublin and has no awareness of how soon and how traumatically he will be summoned back.

It also seems suitable that Stephen's diary should be written in the spring, given the euphoria and sense of new life which color many of its entries. Spring in the northern hemisphere is often regarded as beginning on 20 March, which may be one reason why the diary opens on that particular day. Moreover, 20 March is the birthday of Ibsen, a writer Joyce took as a model in his quest to free Irish society from its collusion in colonial oppression, among other things. (We know that Joyce knew this date, since he had once sent Ibsen a birthday message which earnestly combined sincere congratulations for Ibsen with equally sincere approbation for himself.) Stephen may share Joyce's wish to become Ibsen's successor, since earlier in *A Portrait* he has anticipated how "the spirit of Ibsen would blow through him like a keen wind, a spirit of wayward boyish beauty" (*P* 176). And, as Michael Levenson has noted in his astute account of Stephen's diary, 20 March is also the date of the initial diary entry in Turgenev's novella *The Diary of a Superfluous Man*, which we know Joyce had read, and which has a few points of congruity with *A Portrait*—for example, the tone in which one day's diary entry will sometimes denigrate the previous day's entry.[1] Various mild ironies seem to be directed at Stephen through his choice of a date to begin his diary, whichever of these connotations Joyce had primarily in mind.

On the face of it, though, Stephen starts the diary in order to reflect, in a rather "literary" way, on a conversation he has just had with his friend Cranly that appears in the novel's text immediately before the diary begins. In that conversation Stephen speaks of resisting his mother's pleas that he should be a good Catholic and make his Easter duty. His first diary entry for 20 March begins, "Long talk with Cranly on the subject of my revolt" (*P* 247). Stephen appears to have written this account on the day of the conversation: that would be consistent with his practice of recording each day's activities in his later diary entries. We can therefore date precisely a lengthy section of the

---

1. Michael Levenson, "Stephen's Diary: The Shape of Life," in *Critical Essays on James Joyce's "A Portrait of the Artist as a Young Man,"* ed. Philip Brady and James F. Carens (New York: G. K. Hall, 1998), p. 41.

novel's fifth chapter, covering twenty-four pages in the Viking edition, or about ten percent of the novel. This section, which stretches from Stephen's villanelle-writing scene to his first diary entry, is set on a single day, which we can thus be confident is Friday, 20 March 1903. Amusingly, Stephen's highly crafted villanelle, which is presented in full in the novel, ends with the line "*Tell no more of enchanted days*" (*P* 224). Only one day then separates it in the novel's text from the diary, which records numerous days, enchanted and otherwise.

As for the other dates within the diary, a few connotations and patterns are discernible. Since we know when Easter fell in 1903, we might notice that the diary entries clustered around the time of Easter seem apt in their brooding and then aspiring moods, even though no specific allusion to events at Easter appears. These reported moods, and the lack of any specific allusion, suggest that Stephen has noted the presence of Easter but has adhered to his uneasy but pointed resolution of not making his Easter duty (which would have entailed going to confession) despite his mother's pleas (*P* 239). Otherwise, there would almost inevitably be some reference to his doing so. Once we know the year, we also know the days of the week, and Joyce obviously paid close attention to such details: for example, Stephen goes to his university classes on a number of the days which have diary entries, but, as far as we can tell, never on a weekend. It also appears that, unlike Joyce, Stephen interrupts his studies in order to head off to the Continent and never completes his university degree. Joyce, as usual, completed and tidied this phase of his life more expeditiously than Stephen.

The diary contains entries for twenty of the thrity-nine days it spans, so on average Stephen records something on only one day out of every two. He is a desultory diary-keeper. He becomes increasingly desultory as time goes on, and the periods without any diary entries tend to become longer and longer: the final entries for 26 and 27 April are preceded by a lengthy run of nine days with no entries at all. Very likely preoccupation with his impending departure is getting in the way of the humdrum activity of diary-writing. In a couple of cases, when Stephen is clearly feeling more energetic than usual, two diary entries appear for a single day. On the morning of 21 March, for example, he punctiliously records a thought he had had the night before, then he adds a further reflection during the same evening (which seems to be the time of day when he usually writes in the diary, just as we might expect, although some of the entries do not reflect specifically on his day's activities). The two entries for 6 April record two views of the relationship of past and future, and they involve images of looking back and forward: content which makes dual entries appropriate.

It may still seem strange that Stephen should keep a diary at all. Joyce never kept one, as far as we know. He mocked Stanislaus for doing so, then stole material from it. Earlier in the fifth chapter, Stephen has shown an affectedly bohemian indifference to mundane realities like clock time and the days of the week. As he walks to the university he hears a clock strike: "Eleven! Then he was late for that lecture too. What day of the week was it? He stopped at a newsagent's to read the headline of a placard. Thursday" (*P* 177). (Presumably, though, he remains sufficiently in touch with reality that he knows not to head off to classes on a weekend.) The neatly dated diary entries at the end of the same chapter imply that he has become mentally better organised now that he is sorting out his departure from Dublin rather than lazily following, or failing to follow, his lecture timetable. The diary also seems to recapitulate and to tidy material which has already been presented throughout the novel, and especially within the fifth chapter itself, to "put it in order" as Stephen's mother does with his new secondhand clothes (*P* 252). All the major scenes of depicted action early in the fifth chapter are systematically recalled by scenes within the diary itself: early in the chapter and again in the diary, two scenes are set at the National Library, two scenes in the street, one set at the university, one showing Stephen in Stephen's Green, and several implicitly (but seldom explicitly) set at Stephen's home. Also, early in the chapter and again in the diary, Joyce depicts significant encounters with each of Stephen's friends: Davin, Lynch and Cranly. While such echoes might suggest a degree of repetition and entrapment, they also show increasing levels of control. Within the diary entries, for example, Stephen mostly presents his own movements through Dublin, and his arrival at the various scenes of action, in a volitional way, which shows him taking possession of his experiences, just as he describes himself "crossing Stephen's, that is, my green" (*P* 249). The exception to this volitional aspect is his final meeting with his sometime girlfriend Emma: "Met her today pointblank in Grafton Street. The crowd brought us together" (*P* 252). He still needs to sort out that side of his life, and it remains unsorted in *Ulysses*.

Fixing the dates of Stephen's diary in the concluding chapter might make us wonder if we can do something similar with other parts of the novel. In fact, the whole of the third chapter can be dated precisely, to just a few days in December 1898, using evidence about the timing of the retreat at which Stephen hears the hellfire sermons. As Hugh Kenner points out, knowledge that the feast day of Saint Francis Xavier fell on a Saturday in 1898 is all we need to fix these dates.[2] This evidence is supported by Stephen's declaration to the priest who hears his confession toward the end of the third chapter, on the day of the final retreat sermon, that his age is sixteen. *Ulysses* reveals that Stephen was born in 1882; hence, he will have turned sixteen by the end of 1898. So we can be quite sure that Stephen's confession takes place on Friday 2 December 1898 and that the communion service depicted at the end

2. Hugh Kenner, *Ulysses* (London: Allen & Unwin, 1980), p. 161.

of the third chapter takes place on Saturday 3 December 1898. It seems striking that Joyce so carefully includes information enabling us to date all the scenes in the third chapter, even if we have not yet ascertained exactly why these dates are significant. Perhaps the very precise and mundane dating interacts ironically with the resonant declarations about eternal punishment that Stephen hears in the sermons. It also shows Stephen's educational career already lagging behind Joyce's, since Stephen is still at school late in 1898, by which time Joyce had left and begun studying at University College. During his confession after the retreat sermons, Stephen reveals another facet of his spiritual evolution: he acknowledges that his previous confession had taken place "eight months" before (*P* 144), which would place it at Easter 1898; so we can assume he was still making his Easter duty in those days.

The easiest piece of the whole novel to date with certainty is the Christmas dinner scene in the first chapter. The first Christmas after the death of Charles Stewart Parnell, the dinner famously turns into a bitter debate focused on Parnell and featuring especially Stephen's father and his aunt Dante. Parnell's death happened in October 1891; hence, the date of the Christmas dinner scene must be 25 December 1891. But we can also go back a little and date the first of the two long scenes set at young Stephen's boarding school, Clongowes Wood College. This is the nineteen-page sequence stretching from the novel's one-and-a-half-page "overture" to the Christmas dinner scene itself. Since the "overture" is impressionistic and dateless, like the overture to Yeats's autobiographical *Reveries over Childhood and Youth* written at about the same time, this initial Clongowes scene is the first extended narrative sequence in *A Portrait* to take place on particular days in the calendar. We can precisely date this second scene in the novel, given that (as shown earlier) we can precisely date the second-to-last scene in the novel, the one that incorporates Stephen's conversation with Cranly and immediately precedes Stephen's diary, and which must take place on 20 March 1903. Joyce worked out a thorough mirror-symmetrical pattern linking the novel's first and last chapters, and the fact that these two particular scenes can be precisely dated serves as one of many instances of that pattern. There are several other links between the two scenes as well.

Just a few pages into the novel, very early in Stephen's first term at Clongowes, we learn of his ritual involving numbers pasted inside the lid of his desk. This is his way of counting down to the Christmas holidays: "Soon they would be going home for the holidays. After supper in the studyhall he would change the number pasted up inside his desk from seventyseven to seventysix" (*P* 10). A little later, "sitting in the studyhall he opened the lid of his desk and changed the number pasted up inside from seventyseven to seventysix. But the Christmas vacation was very far away: but one time it would come because the earth moved round always" (*P* 15). And he fantasises about "going home for the holidays! That would be lovely: the fellows had told him. Getting up on the cars in the early wintry morning outside the door of the castle" (*P* 20).

This scene definitely occurs during Stephen's first school term: he has not been home for Christmas holidays before ("that would be lovely: the fellows had told him"). Stephen must, therefore, start school at the age of nine, since it is now late in 1891 and he was born in 1882. If, like Joyce, he was born in February 1882, as we are strongly tempted to suspect, then by late 1891 he would be almost ten. Joyce himself started at Clongowes in mid-1888, at the age of six-and-a-half, and Stephen scarcely seems nine years old in that first Clongowes scene: he appears very small and helpless as the other boys play rugby and he tries to stay out of the action. We should perhaps allow for the fact that Stephen has been pushed into some water the day before and is now coming down with a cold or the flu, or maybe even pleurisy or dysentery, more explicit symptoms of which will appear on the following day. He is also feeling acutely homesick, so during the scene he may be less robust than usual. The minimum age for starting at Clongowes was normally seven, so Joyce did begin a little early, and some pupils did, apparently, join the school at the age of nine. Thus the notion that Stephen is nine years old when he starts at the school is historically plausible. Yet it may not be fully realised in the text, and there seems to be a degree of autobiographical contamination in the depiction of his early schooldays. We might suspect, in this instance, that Joyce hopes readers will not bother to investigate. We notice also that Stephen's ritual of changing the numbers in his desk takes place each evening, and also the historically accurate fact that Clongowes broke up for Christmas early in the morning ("getting up on the cars in the early wintry morning") so that pupils would then have time to reach their homes anywhere in the country in the course of the short Irish winter day. That detail enables us to calculate with reasonable certainty how Stephen is counting the days.

Readers sometimes complain that the dating in the novel's first chapter is vague, or even wonder if Joyce moved the date of Parnell's death back so that it would correspond with his own first term at Clongowes in 1888. Joyce would scarcely do that (although in *Ulysses*, he does have a character misdate the Phoenix Park murders by one year, from 1882 to 1881, and remain uncorrected when he does so). The motive here may have been Joyce's wish to avoid a gratuitous and inauspicious citation of 1882, the year of his own birth and Stephen's). In fact, *Ulysses* reveals that Stephen's aunt Dante moves out of the Dedalus household on a noteworthy and carefully specified date, 29 December 1891 (*U* 17.480). After the conflict at Christmas dinner, then, she no longer feels able to stay, or is perhaps "encouraged" to depart, and she leaves just four days later. So we can be quite confident that Parnell dies on the same date in *A Portrait* as he did historically.

Hans Walter Gabler has investigated at length the implications of Stephen's counting the days during the first Clongowes scene.[3] But he measures back from Christmas Eve to establish the date of that action. In fact, it seems that Stephen is counting down specifically to the end of term, so we should probably measure back from there in order to find the day of the scene when he does his counting. In 1888, when Joyce himself was in his first year at Clongowes, the school broke up for Christmas on 20 December, which was the normal date in the years around that time. (According to the Clongowes Wood College website, in 2006 they broke up on 21 December; this is not a school at which things change very much or very rapidly, though these days they do have a website.) Assuming that 20 December is the date Joyce had in mind for the end of term, the moment when Stephen switches the number in his desk "from seventyseven to seventysix" is likely the evening of 5 October 1891. After Stephen switches the number, one night passes, so it would be 6 October when he becomes ill and goes to the infirmary. Toward evening on that day, he reflects "how pale the light was at the window! ... The fire rose and fell on the wall. It was like waves. Someone had put coal on and he heard voices. They were talking. It was the noise of the waves. Or the waves were talking among themselves as they rose and fell" (P 26). He then apparently has a vision involving Parnell's death and the return of his body to Ireland:

> A tiny light twinkled at the pierhead where the ship was entering: and he saw a multitude of people gathered by the waters' edge to see the ship that was entering their harbour. ... A wail of sorrow went up from the people.
> —Parnell! Parnell! He is dead!
> They fell upon their knees, moaning in sorrow.
> And he saw Dante in a maroon velvet dress and with a green mantle hanging from her shoulders walking proudly and silently past the people who knelt by the waters' edge. (P 27)

Parnell died in England during the evening of 6 October 1891, which, according to these calculations, corresponds to the time of Stephen's vision. Yet the vision itself is obviously prophetic: Parnell's death was not announced until 7 October, so the people whose voices Stephen hears outside the infirmary on 6 October cannot be discussing it. The return of Parnell's body to Ireland, clearly imagined in Stephen's vision, did not take place until 11 October. But synchronising Stephen's vision with the moment of Parnell's

---

3. Hans Walter Gabler, "The Genesis of *A Portrait of the Artist as a Young Man*," in Brady and Carens, *Critical Essays*, pp. 83-112. Further references will be cited parenthetically in the text.

death in this way is powerful, enriches the Christmas dinner scene which follows, and helps to underpin Stephen's self-identification with Parnell. Parnell was ill during the days leading up to 6 October 1891, partly because he had insisted on giving speeches in the rain, and Stephen is ill on the same days, having been pushed into "cold and slimy" ditch water (*P* 10).

Gabler also explores the date of the Clongowes scene in terms of Parnell (107), but difficulties arise when we count back from Christmas Eve rather than from the end of term four days earlier. Using the end of term seems more consistent with the novel's text, and the Parnell patterns work out better. All the same, Stephen's method of counting the days is not absolutely clear, and it is possible that the switch from seventy-seven to seventy-six occurs one day earlier than argued here. It depends whether he includes 20 December in his count of the remaining days, as assumed in the analysis above, or regards it as already part of the Christmas holidays, which seems less likely but is possible. This alternative counting method would place his Parnell vision on 5 October, the eve of Parnell's death, which would still be prophetic and poignant, just fractionally less precise.

Joyce nevertheless created several major difficulties for himself and for the novel when he decided to move the Christmas dinner scene from the second chapter, where it was originally to appear, to the first chapter. Given the awkwardness that resulted from its move, he must have felt a strong compulsion to strengthen the first chapter by shifting this scene into it. It was this change that indirectly led to Stephen's needing to start school at the age of nine, since Joyce became determined to coordinate the debate over Parnell with Stephen's first trip home from school for Christmas, and that is awkward because Joyce seems never to have thoroughly worked through the process of converting schoolboy Stephen from a six-year-old to a nine-year-old. As Gabler points out, in the published novel Stephen's uncle Charles seems older during the Christmas dinner scene in the middle of the first chapter than he does in several passages (supposedly set later in time) at the beginning of the second chapter (103), and the reason is simply that the Christmas dinner was originally planned to follow those passages: when Joyce moved the dinner, he neglected to rejuvenate Charles enough to make the chronological sequence work smoothly. And there are some seriously ragged edges and loose threads left within the second chapter—the scruffiest chapter in the novel—around the place where the scene was removed. It might seem surprising that Joyce left these in such an untidy state, given his usual fastidiousness, but it appears that by this stage he was transferring his attention from *A Portrait* to *Ulysses*. He still exerted himself enough to make sure that *A Portrait* meshes naturalistically with *Ulysses*, however. He was completing *A Portrait* and planning the early episodes of *Ulysses* around the same time, in the middle of 1914.

So, although *A Portrait* seems to cover a period of almost twenty years, it would be more accurate to say that, after the one-and-a-half page "overture," it actually covers only about eleven years, from late 1891 to early 1903. And it does this in a highly episodic fashion. Most of its content, especially in the first, third and fifth chapters, is concentrated into lengthy scenes that occur on a relatively small number of distinct days, possibly as few as fifteen days in total. In fact, we can ascribe more than forty percent of the novel's pages to a few specific and indisputable calendar dates. More separate days may actually be singled out for particular attention within the relatively brief five-page diary than in all the rest of the novel put together. Along with the brusque tone of many of Stephen's diary entries, that comparison may help to explain the sense of remarkably accelerated progress that the diary conveys. For all its occasional tendencies to repeat and recapitulate, the diary does close the novel quite vigorously, and it convincingly heralds Stephen's departure for the Continent.

We can also now see some further parallels between the novel's opening and its close. Stephen's initial countdown of days until the end of term, which begins on the second page of the novel and on the eve of Parnell's death, and which culminates in the Christmas holidays destined to be riven by the debate over Parnell's legacy, is echoed by the countdown to departure represented in the (almost) daily entries in his diary at the end of the novel. This time, however, Stephen is counting down not merely toward a departure from boarding school but toward a flight from Ireland—a more significant escape from a larger entrapment even though, ironically, this "escape" in April 1903 will also prove to be very temporary, just as the 1891 Christmas holidays were. The beginning of *Ulysses* will show him back in Dublin, just as the section after the Christmas dinner scene in *A Portrait* showed him back at Clongowes. While Parnell seemed to Joyce a genuine hero, Stephen's self-identification with him early in the novel has overtones of masochism and martyrdom: even at the time of his Parnell vision, Stephen knew that his family argued about Parnell, and Dante had already told him that, ever since the revelations about his adultery with Kitty O'Shea, Parnell should be regarded as a bad man (*P* 16). Stephen's overblown self-identification with Daedalus at the end of the novel fails to preclude the likelihood of his being more of an impetuous Icarus than an inventive Daedalus, as he himself acknowledges explicitly in *Ulysses*. When in the diary he announces his plan "to forge in the smithy of my soul the uncreated conscience of my race" (*P* 253), there may be implications of forgery as well as of creation (a duality which Joyce may have borrowed from Dickens's *Great Expectations*). Stephen's initial Parisian exile, however grandly conceived, will last only about five weeks—almost certainly a shorter period of time than the thirty-nine days spanned by the diary in which he had foreshadowed and planned this exile. Nonetheless, the diary, in its depiction of Stephen's new level of control over his own life, his ability to choose his own dates rather than being subjected to someone else's timetable, seems an apt measure of the relatively volitional mode of existence he has now attained. Whereas in earlier parts of the novel Stephen was only implicitly the narrator, by the end he has explicitly assumed this role. The precision of his dating, and our ability to establish exactly where and how the diary fits into his life story, considerably enhances our awareness of his development.

The other implication of the dates of the diary involves *Ulysses*. It's important to know that *A Portrait* ends on 27 April 1903 because it helps to explain the backdrop to the later novel and, in particular, to gloss Stephen's experiences, hopes, and moods in the period just before his trip to Paris and his mother's death. While in *Ulysses* Stephen recalls his five-week Paris sojourn in some detail, he says and thinks virtually nothing about the blank period of time, 355 days in all, that has elapsed between his mother's funeral and the day of *Ulysses*. We have to assume that he has spent this time mooching around Dublin, and at some point he has obviously moved into the Martello Tower with Buck Mulligan and found a teaching job at Deasy's school. Beyond that, we know almost nothing. If anything consequential had happened to him during this time, it seems inevitable that he would recall it somewhere. The ending of *A Portrait* backgrounds all these developments. Dating the diary with precision can show us much more clearly how the gap between Stephen's aspirations and the ongoing reality of his life should be measured. It seems especially poignant and ironic that on 26 April 1903 Stephen should tell us of his mother's plaintive prayer "that I may learn in my own life and away from home and friends what the heart is and what it feels" (*P* 252), given our knowledge from *Ulysses* that she will die less than two months later; in fact, her funeral occurs exactly two months after the diary entry for 26 April. If Stephen does learn something about such matters during his brief period of exile, his mother will not be present to witness the results. We can only appreciate the full implications here if we take the time to work out just when Stephen's diary comes to an end.

University of Auckland, New Zealand

IS BELLA COHEN JEWISH? WHAT'S IN A NAME?

AUSTIN BRIGGS

Abstract: The history of Irish name changing suggests that despite her surname Bella Cohen may not be Jewish. Via an effort at a phonetic rendering of the Gaelic "Cadhain" into English, "Cohen" can be an Irish name. In addition, "Cadhain" (Gaelic for "wild goose"), was also "translated" into the English "Barnacle." The connection between Bella's surname and the Irish "Cohen" and "Barnacle" is noteworthy for two reasons. It opens the possibility that Joyce associated Bella with Nora, and the alternative Hebrew and Gaelic antecedents for "Cohen" offer an example of the indeterminate nature of Jewish and Irish identity in *Ulysses*.

As Fritz Senn observed when he reviewed Clare Culleton's *Names and Naming in Joyce*, the subject of Joyce's "naming devices" is so fascinating that "it is hard to avoid talking about Joyce without launching into this area."[1] "What's in a name?" The question from *Romeo and Juliet,* by the author identified by Stephen Dedalus in "Scylla and Charybdis" as "Rutlandbaconsouthamptonshakespeare or another poet of the same name" (*U* 9.866), appears four times in *Ulysses*. The first time, when someone identified as "MAGEEGLINJOHN" asks it, he implies, as Juliet says, that a rose by any other name would smell as sweet, that names have no intrinsic significance (*U* 9.900). Posing the question twice in "Scylla and Charybdis," Stephen argues to the contrary, proposing that Shakespeare encoded his own name in his works and associated his wife Ann and his brothers with characters bearing the same names in his works (*U* 9.927, 9.986). When Stephen repeats the question in "Eumaeus," however, he maintains that names are "impostures," citing the transformations of Cicero to Podmore, Napoleon to Goodbody, and Jesus to Doyle (*U* 16.362). Bloom readily agrees, explaining—as he pushes a "socalled roll" toward Stephen—that his family name was changed (*U* 16.366).

What *is* in a name, or, more specifically, what is in Bella Cohen's name? Until recently, probably like most readers of *Ulysses*, I had assumed that she is Jewish. I accepted Louis Hyman's assertion, in *The Jews of Ireland*, that Bella Cohen is a Jew based on a Jewish Mrs. Cohen listed in *Thom's*

---

1. Fritz Senn, review of *Names and Naming in Joyce,* by Claire A. Culleton, *JJQ* 33 (Winter 1996): p. 293.

Directory as living in the brothel district of Dublin.[2] I nodded in agreement when Marjorie Garber described Bella as a compendium of "parodic traits of the 'Jewess.'"[3] And I thought that Neil Davison made a good deal of sense when he wrote that "Bloom imagines Bella as the feminine element of his own person—Jewish, libidinous, yet now empowered."[4] I began to question my assumption, however, during one of the reading sessions on *Ulysses* that Michael Groden and I moderated at the Cornell Joyce Conference in 2005. At one point, discussion focused on the passage from "Circe" in which Bello threatens to roast Leopold Bloom and eat him for breakfast (*U* 15.2891-902). Bello's declared taste in the passage for "hamrashers" notwithstanding, Mike and I—and, so it seemed, everyone else present in a group of approximately thirty that included many world-class readers of Joyce—agreed that Bella is Jewish. We were thus taken aback when Cóilín Owens asked why we thought so. When I pointed to her surname, he explained that Cohen is not necessarily a Jewish name in Ireland. Since then, I have been questioning Bella Cohen's name.

The given name does not seem Jewish. After all, Lady Gregory was christened Isabella Augusta, one of Joyce's sisters was Eileen Isabel, and the *Wake* offers numerous *-bellas* for incarnations of Anna Livia and her daughter Issy/Isabel/Isabella under such names as Plurabella, Isolabella, Lovabella, Pullabella. Of course, Bella could be a gentile married to a Jew named Cohen, but her "Mrs." does not necessarily mean that she is married, any more than would the more common "Madame" for women in her managerial position, a title that Joyce plays with in his portrait of Mrs. Mooney in "The Boarding House." To be sure, Bella wears wedding rings on her left hand, speaks of having been married to a grandnephew named Cuck Cohen ("the bloody old gouty procurator and sodomite with a crick in his neck"), and mentions "ten or eleven other husbands" as well (*U* 15.3208-10). [5] In a chapter whose wonders include Molly mounted on a camel and Bloom

---

2. Louis Hyman, *The Jews of Ireland from the Earliest Times to the Year 1910* (Shannon: Irish University Press, 1972), p. 168. With Mrs. Cohen, as with many of his entries, Hyman often seems to determine that people are Jewish entirely on the basis of their names.

3. Marjorie Garber, *Vested Interests: Cross Dressing and Cultural Anxiety* (New York: Routledge, 1992), p. 231.

4. Neil Davison, *James Joyce, "Ulysses," and the Construction of Jewish Identity* (New York: Cambridge University Press, 1996), p. 226.

5. The *OED* offers five definitions for "cuck." One is for an obsolete noun that is short for "cuckold." The remaining entries, for obsolete verbs, include the following: "to void excrement," which explains why Bloom's seat in his outhouse is called a "cuckstool" (*U* 4.500); and "to punish by setting on the cucking-stool," a device for inflicting pain and humiliation that would attract Bella. Don Gifford and Robert J. Seidman's note to "cuckstool" offers the punishment device rather than the more

as the mother of eight sons, however, these claims do not necessarily constitute reliable evidence.

Putting aside Bella's surname for the moment, consider the stage direction for her first entrance in "Circe." It may suggest a Jewish woman when it describes her "olive face" (*U* 15.2747), especially as Bloom is also described as having "an olive complexion" (*U* 17.2003). But many gentiles have such coloring. The ice cream vendor Antonio Rabaiotti; Joseph Nannetti, the foreman at *The Freeman's Journal*; and Stephen's music teacher Almidano Artifoni might all be olive-skinned, but there is no reason to assume that they are of Jewish rather than Italian extraction. In the first edition of his biography of Joyce, Richard Ellmann identified Bloom's possible original, Alfred H. Hunter, as "a dark complexioned Dublin Jew" (*JJI* 238); in the second edition, Hunter is only "rumored to be Jewish" and "putatively Jewish," and Ellmann is silent on the issue of skin tone (*JJII* 162, 230). (Ellmann himself was Jewish but not—as I recall— notably olivaceous.)

The same stage direction also describes Bella as "fullnosed," and when the loungers in "Cyclops" make an anti-Semitic reference to a man "of the bottlenosed fraternity," one can assume that for them there must be such a sorority as well (*U* 12.1086). A large nose is no infallible marker of Jewish ancestry, however: Jimmy Durante, Cyrano, and Pinocchio were apparently all gentiles. Indeed, Bloom may well have a full nose, given the care he takes to avoid showing his profile to Gerty MacDowell, who greatly admires Reggie Wylie's "exquisite nose" and wishes she could see whether her mystery man on the beach has "an aquiline nose or a slightly *retroussé*" (*U* 13.141, 13.420). But surely, unless he is under cover or in deep denial, the citizen is not Jewish, though he is described—in a parodic passage, to be sure—as large nosed to such an extent that within the "cavernous obscurity" of his nostrils "the fieldlark might easily have lodged her nest" (*U* 12.160-61).[6]

But the surname? Surely *Cohen* is unmistakably Jewish. If the Abie of *Abie's Irish Rose* had been an O'Shea instead of a Cohen, or if the five Hollywood features in the *The Cohens and The Kellys* series produced between 1926 and 1932 had been about the Kenners and the Kellys, audiences would have entered theaters with markedly different expectations. Regrettably, when he wrote "Cohen Owes Me Ninety-Seven Dollars," an unpleasant 1916 comic number about a businessman who, even on his

likely seat for voiding excrement (*"Ulysses" Annotated: Notes for James Joyce's "Ulysses,"* rev. ed. [Berkeley: University of California Press, 1988], p. 81); Joyce would have enjoyed the stool/excrement play.

6. Does Stephen have a distinctive nose? He remembers his anxiety in Paris that he might be arrested for murder: "Other fellow did it: other me. Hat, tie, overcoat, nose" (*U* 3.182).

deathbed, can't stop complaining about money owed him, Irving Berlin must have anticipated that those who heard the song would take both the speaker and Cohen to be Jewish.[7] Indeed, what could be more Jewish than *Cohen*? Like such variations as *Cohn* and *Kohn*, it is derived from the Hebrew for "priest, " a descendant of Aaron, bother of Moses.

In *The Stigma of Names*, his study of name branding in Germany from 1812 through 1933, Dietz Bering terms *Cohn* "the surname with the strongest antisemitic charge." He records that as early as 1859 it was argued that a Prussian petitioner should be allowed to change his name from Cohn because the name was "specifically Jewish" and therefore "not very suitable for a judicial officer";[8] another Cohn, seeking to change his name in 1903, noted a derisive turn-of-the-century musical hall number, *Kleine Cohn*, which, Bering records, became so great a hit that anti-Semitic jokes, cartoons, post cards, and songs featuring Little Cohn were widely circulated with increasingly virulence well into the Nazi era (150-52). By 1910, a Berlin lawyer could plead on behalf of a client seeking a name change that *Cohn* had developed "into a term of slander and abuse," a term "used to insult and to deride Jews." "One calls a Jew 'Cohn,'" the lawyer explained, "if one does not know his name or simply wishes to designate him as a Jew" (Bering 149-50).

Stephen is right, however: names *can* be impostors. The discussion of Shakespeare in "Scylla and Charybdis" rests partly on the once-standard biography by Sidney Lee, or, as Mr. Best remarks, by "Mr Simon Lazarus as some aver his name is" (*U* 9.419-20). And, in truth, before changing his name, Sidney Lee was Solomon Lazarus Levi.[9] Bloom's father changed the family name to something less foreign sounding in Ireland. translating Virag—Hungarian for "flower"—to Bloom.[10] Such Jewish name changes

7. Alex Williams, "Love 'Springtime for Hitler'? Then here's the CD for You," *New York Times*, 29 Oct. 2006, Arts section, late edition, p. 1.

8. Dietz Bering, *The Stigma of Names: Antisemitism in German Daily Life, 1812-1933* (Ann Arbor: University of Michigan Press, 1992), p. 149. Further references will be cited parenthetically in the text.

9. Alan Stewart, "The Lives of Roderigo Lopez, Solomon Lazarus Levi and Sidney Lee," *EnterText* 3 (Spring 2003), http://www.brunel.ac.uk/4042/entertext3.2/stewart.pdf (accessed 25 July 2008). Gifford and Seidman incorrectly state that Sidney Lee was originally named Solomon Lazarus Lee (192).

10. Two native-Hungarian colleagues—Tekla Mecsnóber and Ivan Marki—inform me that in late nineteenth- and early twentieth-century Hungary, the German sounding *Blum*—pronounced "Bloom"—was often "Hungarianized" or "magyarized" into *Virag* (Tekla Mecsnóber, e-mail to author, 9 Nov. 2006; Ivan Marki, telephone interview, 8 Dec. 2006). In "'Inbursts of Maggyr': Joyce, the Fall, and the Magyar Language," Mecsnóber proposes that one of Bloom's forefathers would "in all probability" have been *Blum* before changing the name to *Virag* (*Focus: Papers in*

often elicited disapproval and anxiety. The remark about "the bottlenosed fraternity" in *Ulysses*, for example, is made in relation to a scoundrel who "went by the name of James Wought alias Saphiro alias Spark and Spiro" (*U* 12.1086). H.L. Mencken, who once wrote that the Jews could "very plausibly" be termed "the most unpleasant race ever heard of,"[11] noted in *The American Language* that Jews in the U.S. made themselves less noticeable by such changes as "*Cohen* into *Cohn, Cahn, Kann, Coyne,* and *Conn.*"[12] Exposing Jewish "camouflage" in "The Gentle Art of Changing Jewish Names," Henry Ford's anti-Semitic *Dearborn Independent* revealed "the many forms that the priestly name of Cohen takes": *Druce, Freeman, Montague, Cooke,* etc. "It is not to be wondered at," the magazine advised, "that the young lawyer should become Attorney Cohane (which does all the better if thereby certain Irish clients are attracted)."[13] The Nazis promoted a book written by a kindergarten teacher to alert little children to the Jewish foxes trying to hide in their midst. Under a vile illustration, the primer warned,

> So that the Jew will not be known
> He soon renamed himself as shown.
> . . . .
> But very humbly we assume
> A Jew will change his name to Blum.[14]

Jewish name changing was by no means always voluntary, of course. Jews living in the Austro-Hungarian empire were required to take German surnames in 1788, and Jews living under Napoleon had to take surnames in 1808. Forced name changing was common in Ireland as well. From the latter half of the seventeenth century on, countless Irish men and women had to

English Literary and Cultural Studies [Pécs, Hungary: University of Pécs, 2002], p. 4).

11. Terry Teachout, *The Skeptic: A Life of H. L. Mencken* (New York: HarperCollins, 2002), pp. 247-48.

12. H.L. Mencken, *The American Language*, rev. ed. (New York: Knopf, 1921), p. 335.

13. "The Gentle Art of Changing Jewish Names," *The Dearborn Independent,* 12 Nov. 1921, http://www.jrbooksonline.com/Intl_Jew_full_version/ij70.htm (accessed 11 July 2008).

14. These lines, from a book by Elvira Bauer, are quoted in translation in Bering, *Stigma of Names,* pp. 232-33, along with twenty-two additional lines of the scabrous poem and two illustrations for it. The original, *Trau Keinem Fuchs auf grüner Heid und keinem Jud bei seinem Eid* ("Don't Trust a Fox in a Green Meadow or the Oath of a Jew"), reads, *Darf ganz bescheiden tauschet um/Den Namen sich ein Jud auf Blum* (Nürnberg: Stürmer-Verlag, 1936).

take English names for the benefit of non-Irish speakers. Anglo-Irish officials generally anglicized Irish names phonetically, rendering them as they heard them pronounced, without regard to the Irish spelling (which was wildly irregular anyway), a practice that frequently produced numerous versions of the same name.[15] Early in *The Wind that Shakes the Barley*, Ken Loach's 2007 film of the Irish rebellion and civil war in the 1920's, how severe the penalty could be for not anglicizing an Irish name is wrenchingly dramatized when an English patrol murders a young Irishman because he refuses to give his name in English. The forced and voluntary transformations and distortions of Irish names over the centuries produced some remarkable results: *Anguish* (probably from *Angus*) and *Junk* (probably from *Junkum*, a variant of *Jenkins*), as well as such Dickensian delights as *Slush*, *Twaddle*, and *Crank*.[16] Many a Shem and Sean became James and John, though, as far as I know, none outside of *Finnegans Wake* became Justius and Mercius.

All of which leads back to Bella Cohen and the observation of Cóilín Owens that *Cohen* can be an Irish name. Discussing common confusions over Jewish names in Ireland, Ira Nadel in *Joyce and the Jews* cites people named Harris, Baker, and Sinclair as examples of Dublin Jews with Irish sounding names, but he mentions no Jewish-sounding names that trace back to the Celtic clans.[17] Yet there were in Ireland—and there are to this day— Cohens who are as Irish as the Levys who were once Dunlevys.[18] Irish-American Coans researching their family name on the web are doubtless pleased to find a site that offers an impressive coat of arms and a family tree that traces their ancestors back to one Caomhain, "who was chief of the clan in the year 876 AD." They may be surprised, however, to find among the many forms of their patronymic the Jewish-sounding Cohen.[19] In fact, according to Ida Grehan's 1997 *Dictionary of Irish Family Names*, Cohen is "more usually" an Irish than a Jewish surname in Ireland.[20]

To the list of the Irish variants *Coan*, *Coen*, *Cohen*, *Coyne*, and *Kyne* must be added Nora's patronymic name *Cadhain*, pronounced "Kyne" and originally *O'Cadhain*.[21] The transformation of *Cadhain* to *Barnacle* came

15. Edward MacLysaght, *Irish Life in the Seventeenth Century* (Cork: Cork University Press, 1950), pp. 118-21.

16. Edward MacLysaght, *A Guide to Irish Surnames* (Dublin: Helicon, 1964), p. 11.

17. Ira Nadel, *Joyce and the Jews: Culture and Texts* (Iowa City: University of Iowa Press, 1989), p. 146.

18. "The Distortion of Irish Surnames," http://www.heraldry.ws/info/article08.html (accessed 11 July 2008).

19. "Coan Surname Resource Center," http://csrc.homestead.com/coan_genhistory. html (accessed 29 May 2007).

20. Ida Grehan, *The Dictionary of Irish Family Names* (Boulder, Colorado: Roberts Rinehart, 1997), p. 72.

21. Grehan, *Dictionary*, p. 72.

49

about by way of a practice that began in the eighteenth century and extended into the nineteenth when many Irish abandoned phonetic renderings of their names and adopted more English-sounding forms that were supposedly translations of the originals. *O'Brucain*, for example, became *Banks*, *O'Marcy* became *Ryder*, and *O'Malachy* became *Blessing*.[22] (Had Buck, who likes to play the priest, been "Blessing Mulligan," he would surely have had good sport with his name.)[23]

Others writing on Joyce have noted that *Cadhain*—Gaelic for "wild goose"—was changed into *Barnacle* after the barnacle goose, a bird once believed to mature in the water after hatching from shells that grew on trees.[24] Readers who have experienced such changes as "metempsychosis" into "met him pike hoses" (*U* 8.112) and have worked their way through Stephen's "God becomes man becomes fish becomes barnacle goose, becomes featherbed mountain" (*U* 3.477-79), as well as the transformations of the *Wake*, should not find themselves unduly troubled to find that *Cadhains* became *Cohens* and *Barnacles*, that Nora Barnacle might have been Nora Cohen. Prompted by one of Joyce's notes for the *Wake*, "glorious name of Irish Goose," Brenda Maddox proposes that "the Barnacle-Cadhain-seabird connection is one that he [Joyce] would have made";[25] similarly, one

22. Michael O'Brien, "Changes in Irish Names," *Journal of the American Irish Historical Society* X (1911): p. 133.

23. Buck mocks Stephen's surname—"An ancient Greek! (*U* 1.34)—but admits that his own name, Malachi Mulligan, is absurd as well, though he does think that the tripping meter gives it "a Hellenic ring" (*U* 1.42). Dactyls or not, *Malachi* seems thoroughly Irish, presumably going back to the twelfth-century Bishop of Armagh Saint Malachy (*Catholic Encyclopedia*, s.v. "St. Malachy," http://www.newadvent. org/cathen/09565a.htm [accessed 7 September 2007]). Even here, however, complexity surfaces: "Malachi" is the name of the Hebrew prophet whose book closes the Old Testament.

24. Among those writing about Nora who have noted the origin of Barnacle in Cadhain are Cóilín Owens in "The Mystique of the West in Joyce's 'The Dead,'" *Irish University Review* 22 (Spring-Summer 1972): p. 91; Eilís Dillon in "The Innocent Muse: An Interview with Maria Jolas," *JJQ* 20 (Fall 1982): pp. 34-35; Brenda Maddox in *Nora: The Real Life of Molly Bloom* (Boston: Houghton Mifflin, 1988), pp. 9-10; Ira Nadel in *Joyce and the Jews*, p. 145; and Claire Culleton in *Names and Naming in Joyce* (Madison: University of Wisconsin Press, 1994), p. 55. Maddox notes, "The way people in Galway still pronounce it—'Bearnacle'—carries a whiff of the origins of the bird's name: *bernekke* in Middle English and *bernaca* in medieval Latin" (10). Was Joyce aware—as is Margaret Atwood in her *Penelopiad*— that *penelopeia* means "duck" in classical Greek?

25. Maddox, *Nora*, p. 10. Joyce's note can be found in Thomas Connolly, ed., *James Joyce's Scribbledehobble: The Ur-Workbook for "Finnegans Wake"* (Evanston, Illinois: Northwestern University Press, 1961), p. 14. A "grey barnacle

can reasonably speculate that Joyce would have made the *Cadhain-Cohen* connection.

The connection between Bella Cohen's surname and the Irish *Cohen* and *Barnacle* is noteworthy for two reasons. Most obviously, it opens the possibility that Joyce associated Bella with Nora. Perhaps it is significant that one of the two appearances of "barnacle" in *Ulysses* includes barnacle geese in a list of "birds of prey," not a bad description of Bella Cohen (*U* 15.4665). Bella and Nora are certainly linked via the cruelties that Bella/Bello inflicts on Bloom and the sadomasochistic passages in the notorious letters Joyce wrote to Nora when they were separated in 1909: "I would like to be flogged by you. I would like to see your eyes blazing with anger," he writes in September (*SL* 166). By December he is fantasizing an elaborate scenario in which Nora, "like an angry nurse," throws him over her lap and pulls down his trousers in order to "flog, flog, flog me viciously on my naked quivering flesh" (*SL* 188-89).[26]

Furthermore, the alternative Hebrew and Gaelic antecedents for *Cohen* offer an additional example of the indeterminate nature of Jewish and Irish identity in *Ulysses*. Reuben J. Dodd, the moneylender of "the tribe of Reuben" (*U* 6.251), is referred to as "blackbearded Iscariot" and "wandering jew" (*U* 15.1918, 15.2145), and Bloom thinks of him as "really what they call a dirty jew" (*U* 8.1159). Indeed, Dodd does seem unmistakably intended to be Jewish, but as has long been recognized, he may not be so. Bernard Benstock believes that Bloom, "like everyone else in Dublin knows that Reuben J. Dodd is not a Jew."[27] Robert Boyle and Patrick McCarthy, resting their arguments heavily on the life of the historical Dodd, maintain that Joyce's fictional character should be read not as a Jew but as a gentile who behaves like the Jew of anti-Semitic prejudice.[28] And Neil Davison, in *James Joyce, "Ulysses," and the Construction of Jewish Identity*, writes, "through the equivocal nature of Dodd's identity in *Ulysses*, Joyce reties the knot for his readers that he himself had already learned to untie."[29] Whatever the real

gander" appears in *FW* 399.9-10, and "barnacled" appears in the same sentence as "sygnus the swan" in *FW* 423.22.

26. Even those repulsed by such talk might find something endearing in the moment Joyce interrupts this fantasy to say, "Pardon me, dear, if this is silly" (*SL* 189).

27. Bernard Benstock, "Leopold Boom and the Mason Connection," *JJQ* 15 (Spring 1978): pp. 259-62.

28. Robert Boyle, "A Note on Reuben J. Dodd as 'a Dirty Jew,'" *JJQ* 3 (Fall 1965): pp. 64-66. Patrick McCarthy, "The Case of Reuben J, Dodd," *JJQ* 21 (Winter 1984): pp. 169-75. Robert M. Adams contends that Joyce made the fictional Dodd Jewish as an act of revenge against a gentile who "had loaned money to John S. Joyce and, curiously, expected repayment" (*Surface and Symbol* [New York: Oxford University Press, 1962], p. 105).

29. Davison, *James Joyce*, p. 60.

Dodd was, and whatever everybody in Dublin once knew, the question of whether to read the fictional Dodd as Jew or gentile remains a puzzle.[30]

Such indeterminacy surfaces in *Ulysses* as early as the second chapter. Although Mr. Deasy crows that Ireland never let in the Jews, he can be read as a miserly Jew of anti-Semitic caricature treasuring his shekels. Lecturing Stephen on the need to save because "[m]oney is power" (*U* 2.237), he proudly show off "his strongroom for the gold," a savings box sectioned to sort out his crowns, sixpence, and other coins into their various denominations (*U* 2.212). And how is one to read the lapidary Russell? *Russell* is not a Jewish name, but this "[g]randfather ape" gloating over a "stolen hoard" is described as turning over a gem he holds in "vulture nails" to "the point of his Moses beard" (*U* 10.813-14).

Most important, of course, are questions that have long occupied readers of *Ulysses* concerning the "Jewishness" of Leopold Bloom, the uncircumcised, pork-eating, baptized son of a gentile mother and a Jewish father who converted to Catholicism. Numerous articles and entire books— Ira Nadel's *Joyce and the Jews*, Neil Davison's *James Joyce, "Ulysses," and the Construction of Jewish Identity,* and Marilyn Reizbaum's *James Joyce's Judaic Other*—have been devoted to determining what Joyce believed "Jewishness" to be.[31] Opinions range. Irwin Steinberg, for example, not only denies that Bloom is Jewish but asserts that Joyce is anti-Semitic.[32] James Heffernan, though acknowledging the many ways in which Bloom is "anything but orthodox or kosher," maintains that Bloom's "Jewishness is a kind of DNA written into his blood—a racial stamp that he can never erase.[33] Moreover, Bloom himself seems uncertain: in "Cyclops" he identifies himself as Jewish, but in "Eumaeus," telling Stephen of the brush-up with the citizen, he says that "in reality" he is not (*U* 16.1085). Focusing on what he terms "Joyce's uncertainty principle," Phillip Herring becomes impatient with the question: "a very great amount of effort has gone into trying to decide whether or not Leopold Bloom is really Jewish," he says, "when any

30. Connecting characters in *Ulysses* with their originals in life can be tricky. Ellmann relates that the fictional Almidano Artifoni was named after the Director of the Berlitz School in Trieste but modeled on Joyce's Italian teacher at University College Dublin, the Jesuit Fr. Charles Ghezzi (*JJII* 60).

31. Marilyn Reizbaum, *James Joyce's Judaic Other* (Stanford: Stanford University Press, 1999).

32. See Irwin Steinberg's "James Joyce and the Critics Notwithstanding, Leopold Bloom Is Not Jewish," *Journal of Modern Literature* 9 (1981–82): pp. 27–49 and "The Source(s) of Joyce's Anti-Semitism in Ulysses," *Joyce Studies Annual* 10 (1999): pp. 63-84.

33. James Heffernan, "The Story of a Modern Masterpiece," in *Joyce's "Ulysses": Lecture Transcript and Course Guidebook*, Part 1, Lecture 1, The Great Courses, Course no. 237 (Chantilly, Virginia: The Teaching Company, 2001), p. 9.

answer obviously depends on definitions about which there is no consensus and never can be."[34] Perhaps one should be guided by something else Herring says: "Indeterminacy of character in the Joycean sense means that in some important way a character cannot be what he/she is."[35]

The attacks on Bloom as a foreigner in the "Cyclops" chapter should caution against the way I have been speaking of "Irish names" and "Jewish names." Joyce's own surname derived from the French, and his father and a brother bore given names after the Polish Saint Stanislaus Kostka (*JJII* 12-13). Stephen's Greek-sounding surname is an issue in the *Portrait*. Nasty Roche asks Stephen at the very opening of the novel, "What kind of a name is that?" (*P* 9), and, much later, Davin asks, "What with your name and your ideas . . . Are you Irish at all?" (*P* 202). Neither *Virag* nor *Bloom* is an "Irish name," but Leopold Bloom—though the son of a father born a Hungarian Jew—is, of course, Irish. An Irish Ulysses, he is fit to stand beside Cuchulin and Maeve, not to mention Brian Confucius, Dante Aligheri, the Mother of the Maccabees, Muhammad, the Queen of Sheba, the Rose of Castille, Julius Caesar, Alessandro Volta, and all the other Irish whose images are graven on the sea stones that dangle from the girdle of the citizen as ancient Gael. The wonderful list of those stones picturing "the tribal images of many Irish heroes and heroines of antiquity" must be read in two ways (*U* 12.175-76): from one perspective, it mocks the absurdity of a chauvinism that claims all things of value to be Irish; from another, however, it offers a reminder that Ireland, like every other nation, is heir to many other nations and peoples. *Ulysses,* after all, is the child not only of Dublin born and bred James Joyce but also of a far-fling lineage that includes such ancestors as Homer, Shakespeare, and Dante.

In "Ireland, Island of Saints and Sages," the address he gave at Trieste's Università Popolare in 1907, Joyce spoke of an Irish parliamentary candidate who had recently attacked an opponent for being the descendant of an English settler. The rebuke deserved the laughter it had evoked in the press, Joyce said, for "to exclude from the present nation all who are descended from foreign families would be impossible" (*CW* 162). The "Celtic race," he told his audience, was "compounded of the old Celtic stock and the Scandinavian, Anglo-Saxon, and Norman races" (*CW* 161). To that list, *Ulysses* adds the "Jewish race." Is Bella Cohen Jewish? The answer is problematic; what is clear, however, is that, whether descended from Aaron brother of Moses or from the King of an Irish clan, she is Irish.

34. Phillip Herring, *Joyce's Uncertainty Principle* (Princeton: Princeton University Press, 1987), xii-xiii. Herring continues darkly—and teasingly: "Close scrutiny will also show that the evidence has been tampered with" (xiii).
35. Herring, *Joyce's Uncertainty Principle*, p. 107.

53

* * *

Let me close with a postscript concerning a film released in 1903 that can be viewed on the web. The director, Billy Bitzer, is remembered today for his brilliant pioneering work as D.W. Griffith's cameraman on *The Birth of a Nation*, but no hint of talent is visible in this three-minute knockabout comedy. The only thing remotely funny about the spectacle is the name of the vaudeville team whose act is recorded: "Levi and Cohen, the Irish Comedians."[36] At a time when ethnic humor was big in show business, it is obvious that Levi and Cohen were two Jews trying for a laugh by claiming to be Irish. Or is it quite so obvious? Quoting the Irish playwright identified in "Cyclops" as Patrick W. Shakespeare (*U* 12.190-91), *Ulysses* asks, "What's in a name?" Levi and Cohen, the Irish Comedians, could, in fact, have been two Irish tumlers fresh off the boat from Dublin whose forefathers were Shem Dunlevy and Sean Cadhain.

Hamilton College, New York

36. G.W. [Billy] Bitzer, dir., *Levi and Cohen, the Irish Comedians* (American Mutoscope and Biograph, 1903), http://www.open-video.org/details.php?videoid= 4773 (accessed 26 July 2008).

STEPHEN DEDALUS'S ANTI-SEMITIC BALLAD: A SABOTAGED CLIMAX IN JOYCE'S *ULYSSES*

MARGOT NORRIS

Abstract: Stephen Dedalus' singing of "Little Harry Hughes," an anti-Semitic ballad, to Leopold Bloom at the climax of their meeting and perhaps of the book is a seemingly uncharacteristic attack on his undeserving, kindly host. It interrupts the arc of their growing intimacy, complicates our reading of Stephen, and confounds and confuses any satisfactory resolution to their relationship. It also offers a new way of thinking about why Stephen refuses Bloom's offer to spend the night and perhaps become a boarder in his home.

What is the narrative climax of the meeting of Leopold Bloom and Stephen Dedalus in the closing chapters of James Joyce's *Ulysses*? It depends, perhaps, on the definition of "narrative climax." Gerald Prince's *Dictionary of Narratology* calls it "[t]he point of greatest tension; the culminating point in a progressive intensification,"[1] but Wayne Booth cautions us that a narrative climax may not always be self-evident. To the question of "How can an author achieve dramatic intensity?" he adds the question: "How can an author make sure that his most important dramatic moments will be heightened rather than obscured by their surroundings?"[2] This is, of course, the difficulty in Joyce's "Ithaca" chapter, where the rhetoric of catechism frequently obscures rather than elucidates what is going on between Bloom and Stephen. And perhaps this obfuscation muddies and even conceals the moment one could posit as a climax in *Ulysses*: Stephen Dedalus singing an anti-Semitic ballad to Leopold Bloom in the kitchen of his host. The ballad of "Little Harry Hughes," based on the legend of the ritual murder of "little" Hugh of Lincoln, tells of a Jew's daughter who punishes a little boy who broke her home's windows by inviting him into the house and cutting off his head with a penknife. The delivery of this song is excruciatingly problematic

1. Gerald Prince, *Dictionary of Narratology*. rev. ed. (Lincoln: University of Nebraska Press, 2003), p. 14.

2. Wayne C. Booth, *The Rhetoric of Fiction*, 2nd ed. (Chicago: University of Chicago Press, 1983), p. 64. Booth adds a curious footnote to his discussion of dramatic intensification in fiction: "I would not want to be asked for proof, but I suspect that many besides Yeats have praised *Ulysses* as a work of genius without being sufficiently interested even to finish it (see Richard Ellmann, *James Joyce*, p. 545)" (64n63).

on so many counts that it requires considerable discussion to lay them out before its significance can be fully assessed.

Stephen could scarcely doubt that the performance of the song would puzzle, discomfit, and hurt the kindly Bloom who has spent much of the night protecting him from treacherous companions, financial predators, and possible police arrest. The moment, therefore, qualifies as Prince's "point of greatest tension" in the relations between Stephen and Bloom in the novel. But why would Stephen, the antithesis of the anti-Semitic Garrett Deasy, do such a thing? And why would Bloom, after recovering from the impact of the song, nonetheless invite Stephen to spend the night, and perhaps become a boarder in his home? The thematic response to these questions has been heavily conditioned by the Odyssean parallel that casts Bloom and Stephen into the roles of symbolic father and son seeking and finding each other at the end of the story. But such a preemptive scenario obscures the far more complex relationship that emerges if the late development of the relationship is subjected to rigorous scrutiny that simultaneously examines the closing chapters' narratological puzzles. How and why does the narrative strategy of "Ithaca" prevent readers from recognizing not only the significance of the performance of the song, but also its function as a climax of the episode, and perhaps even of the novel's action? These questions speak to the curious lack of mention of the ballad of "Little Harry Hughes" in important early criticism of the episode—an omission particularly remarkable given that Joyce conspicuously reproduced the ballad's musical notation and lyrics *in his own hand* in the text.[3] While a narratological analysis cannot entirely resolve all of these questions, it nonetheless dilates Joyce's efforts to bring his unconventional novel to an ambiguous and ultimately unsentimental conclusion.[4]

---

3. A. Walton Litz, in his influential 1974 essay on the "Ithaca" episode, argues that "both the action and the stylistic development of *Ulysses* reach a climax in 'Ithaca'" ("Ithaca," in *James Joyce's "Ulysses": Critical Essays*, ed. Clive Hart and David Hayman [Berkeley: University of California Press, 1977], p. 386). But in the ensuing discussion of the episode's formal and generic experimentalism, Stephen's singing of the ballad is not mentioned as playing a role in its climax, and is, in fact, not mentioned in the essay at all. Bloom and Stephen's simultaneous urination in the garden constitutes for Litz "the moment of symbolic union" (401) in "Ithaca." But this moment does not fit Prince's and Booth's sense of narrative climax as a point of great tension or dramatic intensity.

4. Much of the difficulty posed by the performance of Stephen's ballad rests on determining precisely what *happens* and what is actually *said* in the episode. The branch of narratology that specifically explores such referential issues is "possible worlds theory," whose premises Gerald Prince describes as follows: "Narratives comprise temporally ordered sequences of states of affairs that are taken to be actual/factual ('what happens') and that are linked to other states of affairs considered

Karen Lawrence, who addresses the episode's narrative strategies, concedes that Joyce deliberately "sets the task for himself of sabotaging the climax" in 'Ithaca,' and even earlier in 'Eumaeus.'"[5] She views this maneuver, however, chiefly as his strategic *tour de force* as a writer: "To abandon the arsenal of literature's weapons, like dramatic climax, tone, style, and linear narration, and still to tell the story is the kind of challenge Joyce enjoyed" (183). But the maneuver also poses challenges to the reader— indeed, *ethical* challenges to judgment and justice—which narrative theory helps to elucidate even though it cannot resolve them. The sabotaged climax in "Ithaca" is produced by what Lawrence calls "a mechanism of avoidance in the narrative" (182), a mechanism that in one of its many forms has the narrative voice withholding crucial information about a character's thoughts or feelings. Instead of telling us Stephen's motives in singing the ballad, the episode's narrative voice—its pretence of omniscience notwithstanding— refuses to address this issue. Such an incomplete construction of a fictional character is not an anomaly, however, but inherent in the condition of fictional-world creation, according to contemporary theorists. "Fictional entities are inherently incomplete," Ruth Ronen writes,[6] and Lubomír Doležel concurs: "Gaps, let us repeat, are a necessary and universal feature of fictional worlds" (169). Wolfgang Iser had earlier pointed to the important function of gaps for engaging the reader interactively with the literary text: "[T]he written part of the text gives us the knowledge, but it is the unwritten part that gives us the opportunity to picture things; indeed without the elements of indeterminacy, the gaps in the text, we should not be able to use our imagination."[7] In the case of "Ithaca," the reader is obliged to compensate for the narrative gap at the episode's climax by producing risky inferences and speculation about the novel's outcome. Joyce's sabotaging of the climax may therefore have an ethical effect, which in turn suggests that

non-actual or counterfactual and constituted by the mental activities of various characters (their beliefs, wishes, plans, hallucinations, fantasies, etc." (77). In the case of "Ithaca" it is not only the mental activities of characters but also those of the anonymous, impersonal narrator that will intervene in the determination of what is factual and what is not factual in the episode. Particularly helpful in exploring the question of factual authentication in narrative is Lubomír Doležel, *Heterocosmica: Fiction and Possible Worlds* (Baltimore: Johns Hopkins University Press, 1998). Further references will be cited parenthetically in the text.

5. Karen Lawrence, *The Odyssey of Style in "Ulysses"* (Princeton: Princeton University Press, 1981), p. 183. Further references will be cited parenthetically in the text.

6. Ruth Ronen, *Possible Worlds in Literary Theory* (Cambridge: Cambridge University Press, 1994), p. 114.

7. Wolfgang Iser, *The Implied Reader: Patterns of Communication in Prose Fiction from Bunyan to Beckett* (Baltimore: Johns Hopkins University Press, 1974), p. 283.

narratorial practices of avoidance, particularly when they concern Bloom's Jewishness, function *performatively* by acting out serious questions whose answers will be far more problematic and ambiguous than any devised by a religious catechism. To examine this effect in "Ithaca" requires that the stakes of the relationship between Bloom and Stephen be dilated in the context of Bloom's earlier experiences on this day—particularly the citizen's anti-Semitic attack on him in Barney Kiernan's pub and its potential future effects on him as a Dubliner.

After reciting an improbably long list of topics that "the duumvirate" of Bloom and Stephen deliberated on their way to Eccles Street, the "Ithaca" narrator asks and answers the question, "Had Bloom discussed similar subjects during nocturnal perambulations in the past?" (*U* 17.46-47). The answer, citing specific conversations in specific years, produces an anomaly that appears to strike Bloom before it strikes either the narrator or the reader: more than ten years have elapsed since Bloom's last meaningful conversation with a friend. "He reflected that the progressive extension of the field of individual development and experience was regressively accompanied by a restriction of the converse domain of interindividual relations" (*U* 17.63-65). In other words, as Bloom's inner life has become richer, his social life has become impoverished. This articulation of Bloom's intellectual and emotional loneliness is most dramatically illustrated when we consider Bloom's options for confiding to someone the events of an earlier narrative climax, namely, the citizen's anti-Semitic assault on him in "Cyclops." In "Ithaca" we learn that he fails to mention "the public altercation at, in and in the vicinity of the licensed premises of Bernard Kiernan and Co, Limited, 8, 9 and 10 Little Britain street" (*U* 17.2252-54) in response to Molly's questions about his day.[8] Yet although he does not confide the incident to his wife, Bloom does confide it to Stephen in the cabman's shelter in "Eumaeus":

> —He took umbrage at something or other, that muchinjured but on the whole eventempered person declared, I let slip. He called me a jew and in a heated fashion offensively. So I without deviating from plain facts in the least told him his God, I mean Christ, was a jew too and all his family like me though in reality I'm not. That was one for him.

---

8. Neil R. Davison suggests the best answer for why Bloom does not tell Molly about the citizen's attack, by pointing out that, in spite of her own possible Jewish heritage, Molly's ruminations on matters Jewish "in no way reveal that she has ever considered herself a Jew" (*James Joyce, "Ulysses," and the Construction of Jewish Identity* [Cambridge: Cambridge University Press, 1996], p. 237). If so, Bloom may be reluctant to share with her evidence of the vulnerability that comes with Jewish identity.

A soft answer turns away wrath. He hadn't a word to say for himself as everyone saw. Am I not right? (*U* 16.1081-87)

This account is reassuring in showing that the citizen's attack did Bloom neither physical nor psychological harm. Indeed, Bloom characterizes himself as the modest victor of the altercation, a view he believes shared by the other men in the pub: "He hadn't a word to say for himself as everyone saw." The reader, privy to the conversation of the men in the pub while Bloom was at the courthouse looking for Martin Cunningham, however, would be obliged to disagree with Bloom's account. It was not only umbrage at Bloom's words, but Lenehan's false information about Bloom's supposedly winning money on the Gold cup race and the resulting insinuation that Bloom was too stingy to stand drinks that incited the citizen's animus. And even Bloom's "friends" in the group betrayed him at a critical moment when a pernicious reputation for tightness and greed was being constructed for him in the pub. The stakes of the events in the pub are therefore far higher than Bloom imagines, and they in turn have a bearing on the significance of his relationship to Stephen Dedalus.

Before looking more closely at this betrayal, I want to consider from a theoretical perspective the significance of two aspects of communicative interaction in groups that form an "agential constellation," as Lubomír Doležel calls it (97). In the pub incident, both cognitive relations ("the knowledge and beliefs of each person about the other members of the agential constellation") and social representations inflected by "attendant collective emotions, such as national, political, or religious fervor, racial and ethnic hatred, and so on" (101) play an important role in how Bloom is perceived. The men in Barney Kiernan's have already been primed by an anti-Semitic intertext, namely Joe Hynes's reference to Shylock, to consider greed and selfishness as stereotypical properties of Jews. Lenehan, who has not heard this part of the conversation, independently applies the stereotype to Bloom when, responding to Martin Cunningham's "asking where was Bloom," he answers, "Defrauding widows and orphans" (*U* 12.1621-22). Lenehan's comment is no more than a quip and is not meant to be taken literally. But when linked to his implication that Bloom is stealthily collecting his Gold cup winnings to avoid standing drinks, it takes on some of the force of a speech act, in the looser sense of that term, as speech "that does something with words."[9] Lenehan's quip is not merely a description by analogy, but an accusation, and it acts performatively to demote Bloom in the eyes of the company if no one comes to his defense. No one does, although Martin Cunningham, the addressee of the quip, knows perfectly well that

9. J. Hillis Miller, *Speech Acts in Literature* (Stanford: Stanford University Press, 2001), p. 1.

Bloom, who has donated an astonishing five shillings to a fund for Paddy Dignam's widow and her five children, qualifies as Dublin's leading benefactor of widows and orphans on this day. Cunningham's "negative semiotic act," or "communicative omission," as Doležel would call it (99), makes him responsible for failing to reverse the stereotype with incontrovertible evidence. Indeed, when Bloom's identity is subsequently raised openly in discussion among the men—"Is he a jew or a gentile or a holy Roman or a swaddler or what the hell is he? asks Ned" (*U* 12.1631-32)—Martin Cunningham gives an unpardonable reply: "He's a perverted jew, says Martin" (*U* 12.1635). The narratorial context of "Cyclops" suggests that this first-person narration is in the process of being circulated by the nameless dun to another group of men in another pub at another time, as David Hayman has argued, at the moment we are reading its account.[10] If so, then the devastating consequences that Cunningham's omission will have on Bloom's reputation become dramatically apparent. Not only does the dun pass on Lenehan's erroneous information with its malicious interpretation, but he further embellishes his narrative with the spiteful stories passed on to him by Pisser Burke, along with his own anti-Semitic commentary. Bloom, who is already a rather isolated loner in Dublin, is in danger of active ostracism in the future. Stephen Dedalus's power to rehabilitate Bloom's maligned reputation takes on critical importance in this context.[11]

To return now to the cabman's shelter, and to Bloom's query to Stephen after confiding his response to the citizen ("Am I not right?"), Stephen concurs only with Bloom's claim that Christ was indeed an Israelite by offering a citation from Paul's epistle to the Romans in the Vulgate. If Bloom sought something more than factual verification of his words and hoped for sympathy—perhaps to have his brave and mature response commended, or for agreement to his pacifistic ideology—he gets no further satisfaction from Stephen. Instead, the pattern of Stephen's response is repeated. Bloom

10. David Hayman, "Cyclops," in *James Joyce's "Ulysses": Critical Essays*, ed. Clive Hart and David Hayman (Berkeley: University of California Press, 1974), p. 241.

11. Phillip F. Herring, ed., *Joyce's Notes and Early Drafts of "Ulysses": Selections from the Buffalo Collection* (Charlottesville: University Press of Virginia, 1977) offers selections from the Buffalo Collection that show that Joyce originally had Stephen Dedalus participate in the anti-Semitic discussion of Bloom in the pub in "Cyclops" (170, 181). Michael Groden points out that Stephen's role in this discussion would have had him "appear in an extremely bad light" (*"Ulysses" in Progress* [Princeton: Princeton University Press, 1977], p. 136). By removing Stephen from "Cyclops" in the final drafts, Joyce deferred Stephen's confusing engagement with anti-Semitism to the direct confrontation with Bloom in the penultimate episode of the book. This deferral prevents readers from pre-judging how Stephen might treat Bloom at the end of their meeting.

continues to inveigh against violence and intolerance: "It's a patent absurdity on the face of it to hate people because they live round the corner and speak another vernacular, in the next house so to speak" (*U* 16.1101-03). Again, Stephen offers only the verification of history by citing examples of seventeenth- and eighteenth-century Dublin factionalism. It is Bloom who offers the kind of hearty agreement and endorsement to Stephen that he would clearly appreciate for his own views: "Yes, Mr Bloom thoroughly agreed, entirely endorsing the remark, that was overwhelmingly right. And the whole world was full of that sort of thing.—You just took the words out of my mouth" (*U* 16.1106-09). Although Stephen has not yet responded to Bloom's more intimate concern with attacks on Jews, Bloom now launches into a spirited defense of Jewish mercantilism as a historical benefit to European nations: "History, would you be surprised to learn, proves up to the hilt Spain decayed when the inquisition hounded the jews out and England prospered when Cromwell, an uncommonly able ruffian who in other respects has much to answer for, imported them" (*U* 16.1120-24). He goes on to offer the socialist impetus behind his own mercantilism, of wanting to see "all creeds and classes *pro rata* having a comfortable tidysized income, in no niggard fashion either, something in the neighborhood of £300 per annum"— a patriotic Irish ideal, as he sees it, "[w]here you can live well, the sense is, if you work" (*U* 16.1133-40). Before Stephen offers his terse *non sequitur* to this lengthy discourse—"Count me out" (*U* 16.1148)—the narrator provides a rare glimpse into Stephen's part in this scene of communication, one that makes it clear that Stephen has heard but not listened.[12] "He could hear, of course, all kinds of words changing colour like those crabs about Ringsend in the morning" (*U* 16.1142-44), but he registers only the words "if you work" and responds with "Count me out." Lubomír Doležel writes, "Communication is an exchange of semiotic acts and, like physical interaction, is reciprocal and can be either symmetrical or asymmetrical" (98). This exchange, which is critical because it may be Bloom's only opportunity to discuss his response to the citizen's attack on him as a Jew with anybody at all, has clearly been asymmetrical, with Stephen barely listening and consequently unresponsive. When Bloom tries to recover from Stephen's seeming rebuff of his argument by including literary labor as an important element in his national project, Stephen steers the conversation into an area of personal bitterness, his conflict with Ireland, ending with his

12. In an early essay on "Eumaeus," Brook Thomas suggests that it may be Bloom's style of discourse that conditions Stephen's lack of responsiveness: "As much as we like to praise Bloom's humanity and classical temper, we become as bored as Stephen and politely try to stifle our yawns when confronted with the style that would produce Bloom's proposed sketch of *My Experiences in a Cabman's Shelter*" ("The Counterfeit Style of 'Eumaeus,'" *JJQ* 14.1 [Fall 1976]: p. 16).

"crosstempered" and impolite, "We can't change the country. Let us change the subject" (U 16.1171). Even if we make allowances for his fatigued and debilitated condition after an exhausting day of disappointment and massive inebriation, Stephen has failed Bloom utterly in this conversation.[13]

This discussion is not the only conversation Bloom and Stephen have in "Eumaeus," but if we return to Prince's definition of narrative climax as "the point of greatest tension," then it may be regarded as the climax of the episode. Bloom's attempt to interest Stephen in the photograph of "Mrs Bloom, my wife the *prima donna*, Madam Marion Tweedy" (U 16.1437), likewise falls flat, although Stephen apparently manages to muster a small compliment on the photo, if not the woman: "Besides he said the picture was handsome which, say what you like, it was, though at the moment she was distinctly stouter" (U 16.1478-80). Given Stephen's lack of response to Bloom's efforts to engage him in topics near to his heart, why does he continue to try? The narrator offers an oblique and ambiguous version of Bloom's own rationalization: "The vicinity of the young man he certainly relished, educated, *distingué*, and impulsive into the bargain, far and away the pick of the bunch, though you wouldn't think he had it in him yet you would" (U 16.1476-78). Stephen's taciturn demeanor leaves open the possibility that under favorable circumstances the potential Bloom senses in him might yet yield the informed, insightful, engaged discussion and exchange that Bloom evidently craves. We saw this need in "Cyclops," where Bloom made a passionate argument for pacifism and tolerance that fell on deaf ears and even ignited the citizen's animus. Bloom needs to talk about both his socialist beliefs and his experiences as a Dublin outsider. At the end of the day, Stephen is his last hope for finding a sympathetic and intelligent interlocutor. And so, after reflecting once more on his little triumph in the pub—"People could put up with being bitten by a wolf but what properly riled them was a bite from a sheep" (U 16.1638-40)—he suggests to Stephen that "you just come home with me and talk things over" (U 16.1644-45). The need to talk is clearly not Bloom's only reason for taking Stephen home with him. Stephen is still quite unsteady on his feet when they leave the cabman's

---

13. Gerald L. Bruns offers a different interpretation of Bloom and Stephen's relationship in this episode. By characterizing Bloom's economic schemes as "not Utopian at all but entrepreneurial, the visions of a would-be *parvenu*," Stephen may be more readily forgiven for offering "sententious and sometimes disagreeable responses" to Bloom's "sorry small talk" ("Eumaeus," in *James Joyce's "Ulysses"*: *Critical Essays*, ed. Clive Hart and David Hayman [Berkeley: University of California Press, 1974], p. 382). Bruns concludes that a "profane silence" surrounds the two men's conversation: "But, after all, it is this profane silence that is the environment of ordinary life, in which such figures as Bloom and Stephen could hardly be expected to do more than sit and speak at an impasse" (382).

shelter, and Bloom knows Stephen has no place to sleep that night—conditions that make it difficult to abandon him on the streets of Dublin after midnight. But then, at the onset of "Ithaca," the tides in Bloom's social fortunes appear to have turned. If this episode's very different narrator could be trusted, Bloom at last reaps a rich conversational reward for his kindness to Stephen on the way back to Eccles Street. In answer to the catechism question, "Of what did the duumvirate deliberate during their itinerary?" (*U* 17.11), no fewer than twenty items are listed, ranging from "Music" to "Stephen's collapse," including literature, friendship, Ireland, Dublin, Paris, women, prostitution, exposed dustbuckets, the Roman catholic church, the study of medicine, and several others.

This list suggests that Bloom's hopeful hunch about Stephen's potential for animated and engaging conversation has been vindicated. Perhaps it has, but this putative talk-fest is such a dramatic turnabout from "Eumaeus" that the reader should be suspicious of the extent to which the seemingly authoritative narrative voice of "Ithaca" can be trusted. The "Ithaca" narrator's reliability long ago snagged on the famous list of Molly's supposed "lovers" (*U* 17.2133-42), which critics were able to "disauthenticate," to borrow Doležel's term (150), by cross-checking the facts with Molly's monologue.[14] But that list is not actually presented as *factual* by the "Ithaca" narrator, who offers it rather as a speculation on a hypothetical thought of Bloom's: "If he had smiled why would he have smiled?" (*U* 17.2126). Sorting out what the "Ithaca" narrator presents as fact and what he does not is crucial to sorting out the question of narratorial authority and reliability in the episode. Lubomír Doležel's discussion of what he calls "authentication functions" offers some helpful insights into the narrator's activity in "Ithaca." Doležel articulates a general rule with respect to truth in narration: "entities introduced into the discourse of the anonymous third-person narrator are *eo ipso* authenticated as fictional facts, while those introduced in the discourse of fictional persons are not" (149). Since the "Ithaca" narrator is clearly both anonymous and impersonal, the reader has no choice but to accept such items as the inventory of Bloom's kitchen dresser (*U* 17.297-318) or the catalogue of books on Bloom's shelf (*U* 17.1361-1407) as factual entities in the fictional world of 7 Eccles Street. But Doležel's caveat about narratorial authentication refers only to facts in fiction, which leaves open the possibility that an anonymous impersonal narrator can nonetheless mislead or produce inadvertent misinterpretations where strict factuality is not at issue. This may be the case with the list of twenty topics the "Ithaca" narrator reports that

14. Robert M. Adams, *Surface and Symbol: The Consistency of James Joyce's "Ulysses"* (New York: Oxford University Press, 1967), pp. 36-40, offers an early review of the quarrels voiced by critics with the list's account of Molly's putative lovers.

"the duumvirate" of Stephen and Bloom "deliberated" on during their walk. Factually we are obliged to trust that twenty topics were indeed broached by the two men. But the narrator's words further imply that Stephen and Bloom formed a coalition to confer and exchange ideas on a series of topics. "Eumaeus" fortuitously offers us a sample of their conversation by giving us a summary of their first discourse on the topic of "Music." But as Paul Schwaber notes, the two men rather "talk past one another."[15] Bloom lays out his musical preferences and judgments, and Stephen, without responding to what he has heard, presents his. Their musical tastes could scarcely be further apart, the conversation suggests, with Stephen sufficiently entranced by the obscure melodies of seventeenth-century English, Dutch, and German lutenists and virginalists to break into a German song by Johannes Jeep. If this musical exchange exemplifies the remaining nineteen topics deliberated by Bloom and Stephen on their journey, the narratorial implication of meaningful conversational engagement is misleading.

What, then, does transpire *factually* between Bloom and Stephen in the Eccles Street kitchen? The narrative voice of "Ithaca" does its best to make this determination difficult. Karen Lawrence notes, "Just as we are hoping for the resolution of the plot, then, the narrative opens up to include almost everything imaginable. In addition to the exhaustive tracing of the causes and effects of events in the plot, the narrative increasingly speculates on potential causes and effects of hypothetical events" (192). We could add the additional complication of the narrative focus on what Gerald Prince calls the "disnarrated": "The elements in a narrative that explicitly consider and refer to what does *not* take place" (22). What is *said* by the men frequently needs to be disentangled from what is *not* said. After Bloom has put the kettle on the hob, he apparently asks Stephen if he would like to wash his hands at the tap. We infer his question from Stephen's negative answer ("What reason did Stephen give for declining Bloom's offer?" [*U* 17.236]), although it is unclear whether Stephen actually articulates his distrust of "aquacities of thought and language" (*U* 17.240) to Bloom. The narrator then tells us what Bloom does *not* say in response—the advice on hygiene he holds back and represses. The precise conversation of the men is therefore often difficult to infer. After pouring their cocoa, Bloom apparently lets Stephen know that he would ordinarily be using Milly's moustache cup and that they are enjoying Molly's cream. Stephen "accepted them [these courtesies] seriously" (*U* 17.368-69), but we do not learn with what words or gestures. Later we receive a summary of earlier encounters between Bloom and Stephen as a child, but it is not until the narrator asks, "Did their conversation on the

15. Paul Schwaber, *The Cast of Characters: A Reading of "Ulysses"* (New Haven: Yale University Press, 1999), p. 182. Further references will be cited parenthetically in the text.

subject of these reminiscences reveal a third connecting link between them?" (*U* 17.477-78), that we can infer that they actually discuss their prior meetings. Clearly they then *do* talk about the relationship each had with "Mrs Riordan (Dante)" (*U* 17.479). But another disnarration soon follows: "Did either openly allude to their racial difference? Neither" (*U* 17.525-26). This topic, for which an opening had been created by Bloom's confidence in the cabman's shelter, is not broached in the kitchen at this time, for reasons that are given in an account of thought exchange so convoluted that it signals chiefly the sensitivity of the topic: "He thought that he thought that he was a jew whereas he knew that he knew that he knew that he was not" (*U* 17.530-31). Instead of discussing ethnicity, the men now describe to each other creative scenarios for advertising and fiction, followed by another significant moment of disnarration. This exchange follows Stephen's delivery of a sketch with a "Hauptmannesque flavor," as Gifford and Seidman call it,[16] of a young man and woman in a remote mountain hotel room that ends with the woman writing something on a piece of hotel stationery. It turns out to be the words "Queen's Hotel, Queen's Hotel, Queen's Hotel" (*U* 17.619-20). Bloom now seemingly refrains from verbally depicting the scene of his father's suicide at the Queen's Hotel in Ennis to Stephen, while Stephen apparently goes on to tell Bloom the little story he calls "*A Pisgah Sight of Palestine* or *The Parable of the Plums*" (*U* 17.640-41). If we recall the Johannes Jeep ballad that Stephen sang to Bloom in German on their walk, a pattern of sorts emerges that shows Stephen chiefly delivering creative or cultural set-pieces to Bloom: the Jeep song, the mountain hotel scenario, his parable, and then "The Ballad of Little Harry Hughes."

Stephen's narration of *A Pisgah Sight of Palestine* to Bloom appears to trigger a series of interchanges that now veer toward the subject of "racial difference" they had earlier avoided. "What statement was made, under correction, by Bloom concerning a fourth seeker of pure truth, by name Aristotle, mentioned, with permission, by Stephen?" (*U* 17.715-17), the narrator asks. The "correction" and "permission" remain obscure, but the answer implies that the title of Stephen's parable prompted Bloom to free-associate the names of three "seekers of pure truth" named "Moses." Hearing mention of Moses Maimonides, Stephen, who had thought about the twelfth-century Talmudic scholar in "Nestor" (*U* 2.158), now appears to mention Maimonides's work, attempting "to reconcile Aristotelian reason and Hebraic revelation" (Gifford and Seidman 576) to Bloom. Bloom responds by bringing up the "Jewish legend," as Gifford and Seidman call it (576), that Aristotle "had been a pupil of a rabbinical philosopher, name uncertain" (*U*

16. Don Gifford, with Robert J. Seidman, *"Ulysses" Annotated: Notes for James Joyce's "Ulysses,"* 2nd ed. (Berkeley: University of California Press, 1988), p. 575. Further references will be cited parenthetically in the text.

17.718-19). At last Bloom appears to receive the kind of intellectually substantive and meaningful conversation he has evidently been craving. The conversation continues promisingly enough, with mention of such other "anapocryphal illustrious sons of the law and children of a selected or rejected race" (*U* 17.720-21) as Mendelssohn, Spinoza, Mendoza, and Lassalle—a heterogeneous list of composer, philosopher, boxer, and Marxist socialist, to be sure, but nonetheless promising discursive material. But curiously the conversation does not continue in this vein, even though Stephen would seem as potentially engaged as Bloom in these topics rife with philosophical suggestion. Instead, they commence a kind of game of Irish and Jewish analogy, producing fragments of ancient Irish and Hebrew verse, Irish and Hebrew "phonic symbols," that culminates in an exchange of songs. It remains unclear why the promising discussion of Jewish figures veers off into this ethnic game, whose irony is, of course, the ambiguous relationship each man has with his ethnic heritage. But the narrator extrapolates from this exercise a virtually transcendent possibility of communion not only between Stephen and Bloom as individuals but also between the Irish and the Jewish people as races with analogous genealogical, cultural, and political histories.[17] "What points of contact existed between these languages and between the peoples who spoke them?" (*U* 17.745-46), the narrator asks, and the list ends with "their dispersal, persecution, survival and revival" (*U* 17.755-56) and "the restoration in Chanah David of Zion and the possibility of Irish political autonomy or devolution" (*U* 17.759-60). Rhetorically, the narrator here shapes a crescendo of communicative possibility that leads to a climax of meaningful understanding and exchange that will take form as a celebration in song. "What anthem did Bloom chant partially in anticipation of that multiple, ethnically irreducible consummation?" (*U* 17.761-62), the narrator asks, and Bloom offers a perfect response with his chant of the anthem of the Zionist movement. Then, in a stunning fracture of the game, and sabotage of the climax, Stephen sings his anti-Semitic ballad.

The ballad of "Little Harry Hughes" was inspired by the story of a Christian boy, Hugh of Lincoln, who was putatively crucified by Jews in 1255 and had his body thrown into a well. In Stephen's variant, little Harry's ball is knocked into a Jew's garden and breaks *"the jew's windows all"* during play with friends. The Jew's daughter urges little Harry to come inside, and, although he demurs, she leads him in, takes a penknife, and cuts

---

17. Ira Nadel notes, "In Ireland, the freedoms and status of the Jews partly resulted from an implicit identity with the persecution the Irish had undergone and the possible historical link between the two people. The Irish, some believed, may have been a lost Semitic tribe" (*Joyce and the Jews: Culture and Text*. [Iowa City: University of Iowa Press, 1989], p. 59).

off his head.[18] This song disrupts the game, as Stephen and Bloom had played it up to this point, of producing analogous Irish and Jewish cultural signs. But the narrator produces an ambiguity with respect to which of the men stops the game. "Did the host encourage his guest to chant in a modulated voice a strange legend on an allied theme?" (*U* 17.795-6), he asks, leaving it unclear what precisely Bloom encourages Stephen to chant. The spirit of the exchanges on Irish and Hebrew matters they have been engaging suggests that Bloom now prompts Stephen to sing an Irish anthem or signature tune, perhaps in Gaelic, in response to Bloom's chanting of *Hatikvah*. This is one construction of an "allied theme." If it is accurate, Stephen's response would seem to violate the spirit of the game, since the provenance of the ballad appears to be British rather than Irish.[19] But if Bloom actually requests "a strange legend," then he could possibly be seen as requesting this specific piece of music. This view seems unlikely on several counts, chiefly because its subject matter is so patently *not* conducive to the ethnic "consummation" Bloom appeared to anticipate with his own Hebrew anthem. If the song is Stephen's choice, then the question arises as to why Stephen selects this song to sing to Bloom at this emotionally promising and charged moment. If the song's impetus were merely its "strange legend," Stephen could have produced a variant titled "Little Harry Hughes and the Duke's Daughter," with alternative wording produced "in genteel avoidance of the ballad's 'anti-Semitism'" (Gifford and Seidman 579). But he unequivocally sings to a Jew who has a daughter the version in which the murderess is the Jew's daughter. To ensure that the reader not miss the implication of the ballad for Bloom as a Jew, the narrator emphasizes it in the questions and answers that follow. "How did the son of Rudolph receive this

18. Five verses of the ballad are cited in the text. Here are the last two:

> *She took him by the lilywhite hand*
> *And led him along the hall*
> *Until she led him to a room*
> *Where none could hear him call.*

> *She took a penknife out of her pocket*
> *And cut off his little head.*
> *And now he'll play his ball no more*
> *For he lies among the dead.* (*U* 17.821-28)

19. Richard Madtes argues that Joyce could have been familiar with an Irish version of the ballad, although the variant he cites as relevant to Joyce's version refers to the "duke's daughter" rather than to the "Jew's daughter" as the murderer of little Harry Hughes (*The "Ithaca" Chapter of Joyce's "Ulysses"* [Ann Arbor: UMI Research Press, 1983], pp. 96-97).

67

first part" (*U* 17.809): "With unmixed feeling. Smiling, a jew, he heard with pleasure and saw the unbroken kitchen window" (*U* 17.810-11). Bloom's initial reaction implies that he is unfamiliar with the ballad and initially untroubled by any intimation of the story's outcome. The question is now repeated after the second part, "How did the father of Millicent receive this second part?" (*U* 17.829), and now Bloom reacts to the song "With mixed feelings. Unsmiling, he heard and saw with wonder a jew's daughter all dressed in green" (*U* 17.830-31). His surprise at the turn of the story confirms that Bloom neither knew nor requested this specific "strange legend" and that the choice was Stephen's.

As the narrator confirms that the entire ballad was chanted by Stephen and that Bloom has heard all of it, the text ensures that, in the event the reader is unfamiliar with the ballad, it is inescapably foregrounded. Not only are all five verses produced in italics, but the first and second verses are produced *again*, in [Joyce's] handwriting, along with their handwritten musical notation.[20] With these marked graphic reproductions, the text conspicuously and aggressively makes it impossible for the reader to miss, misunderstand, or misconstrue the literal wording of the ballad. There is no mistaking the anti-Semitic thrust of the song and no escaping the necessity of dealing with the *fact* that Stephen has deliberately sung it to Bloom. Why has he sung it? The "Ithaca" narrator has access to Stephen's thoughts but does not produce them, and this lack obliges the reader to speculate. What is at stake in the task of constructing an explanation for Stephen's behavior is a matter of ethical judgment. The reader should condemn it as a cruel and unprovoked assault on a gentle man who has been Stephen's protector, benefactor, and caretaker all evening. Nor can Stephen's egregious insensitivity be excused, for Bloom has confided to him both his recent experience as a victim of racial prejudice as well as his sensitivity to the historical persecution of Jews. The ballad, particularly if it is a *non sequitur* in their discussion of Irish and Jewish comparisons, vividly demonstrates to Bloom how deeply embedded anti-Semitism's legacy resides in the cultural repertoire of even such an ostensibly cultivated and enlightened sensibility as Stephen's. And yet a brutal attack on an innocent man is so out of character with everything we have seen of Stephen's thoughts, encounters, and behavior throughout the day that it would seem to be unthinkable. Consequently, critics are prodded to construct psychological justifications for Stephen's act, and in doing so they are obliged to rely on Stephen's only response to his own performance, which takes the form of a "commentary" on the song, inferred from the narrator's

20. Madtes writes, "We know that although the words under the music in the *Ulysses* text were written down by Joyce himself, the musical notation was written by his friend Jacques Benoît-Méchin" (97).

catechism direction: "Condense Stephen's commentary" (*U* 17.833). Here is the condensation:

> One of all, the least of all, is the victim predestined. Once by inadvertence, twice by design he challenges his destiny. It comes when he is abandoned and challenges him reluctant and, as an apparition of hope and youth, holds him unresisting. It leads him to a strange habitation, to a secret infidel apartment, and there, implacable, immolates him, consenting. (*U* 17.834-38)

Had the narrator reproduced Stephen's commentary verbatim and clarified whether it was articulated audibly or represented merely as an internal rumination, the reader could, of course, better judge Stephen's intention and response to the effect he has created. But the reader receives only the narrative synopsis, delivered in what Paul Schwaber describes as "an allegorical mode that abstracts and mystifies" (188). Yet on the basis of this information, or lack thereof, the reader must produce the excruciatingly difficult judgment of what transpires at the climax of this episode. And the narrator confuses the issue further by using the language of his redaction of Stephen's commentary to hint at a veiled interpretation that clarifies nothing at all. Bloom's response to the ballad is to remain sad, still, and silent. "Why was the host (victim predestined) sad?" (*U* 17.838), the narrator asks. But who designates Bloom as "victim predestined," Stephen or the narrator? And what does the term mean? That Bloom can be identified with little Harry as a victim of excessive retaliation? If this is what Stephen means, why does he not say so to Bloom, or why does the narrator not tell us that this is what Stephen means? Again the narrator asks, "Why was the host (secret infidel) silent?" (*U* 17.843), and here Bloom, in contradiction to the earlier designation, seems identified with the Jew whose daughter immolates little Harry Hughes. The answer to this question is Bloom's wide-ranging and thoughtful rumination on "possible evidences for and against ritual murder" (*U* 17.844), a discussion he might have aired with Stephen had the conditions for meaningful conversation with the young man not been shattered.

Given the reader's quandary in judging Stephen's singing of the ballad, it is instructive to survey a small selection of critical response to this moment in "Ithaca," produced over the last several decades. Stanley Sultan relies on the narrator's summary of Stephen's commentary to interpret the ballad as Stephen's "celebration of his deliverance."[21] "He comments on 'Little Harry Hughes' in terms that identify himself as the Christian child and embody that

21. Stanley Sultan, *The Argument of "Ulysses"* (Columbus: Ohio State University Press, 1964; reprint, Middletown: Wesleyan University Press, 1987), p. 390. Further references to the reprint edition will be cited parenthetically in the text.

wonder," Sultan writes (389). Accepting the commentary's invitation to read the ballad allegorically, Sultan finds in it Stephen's tribute to Bloom, who has served as agent for Stephen's return to God: "Not only Stephen and the narrator but also Joyce himself insist that Stephen has in this episode accepted the sacrament offered by God's emissary" (389). The sacrament is Holy Communion, the shared "massproduct" [of cocoa] symbolizing the immolation of Christ, and God's emissary has been Bloom. Sultan's reading of the incident effectively sets aside the song's anti-Semitism as not intended by Stephen. The narrator's summary of the commentary does indeed suggest that Stephen considers little Harry Hughes to have deliberately courted his fate and sought martyrdom at the hands of the Jew's daughter. If so, then the Jew's daughter may be considered exonerated by Stephen were it not for the part which the Israelite's role in Christ's crucifixion has historically played in anti-Semitic logic. But could Stephen really have been oblivious to the ballad's status as a "blood libel" against Jews, whose historical precedent produced the executions of nineteen and imprisonment of ninety Jews in the case of "little" Hugh of Lincoln in 1255? And could Stephen have failed to be aware of the recrudescence of such a blood libel in Chaucer's "Prioress's Tale"? No matter what commentary Stephen produces, he must be aware of his ballad's function as an anti-Semitic intertext in cultural discourse, like the Shylock reference that earlier in the day helped condition a pub full of men to become hateful toward Bloom.

Paul Schwaber makes no excuses for Stephen: "That Stephen, thoughtlessly or not, should sing a strain of Christian anti-Semitism at that moment—the very genre of blood libel that started pogroms—suggests a surge of hostility in him that registers not as affect but as chilling action" (187). But this interpretation leaves Schwaber with the problem of accounting for "Stephen's nastiness" (188) and "staggering rudeness" (187). His solution is to find comfort in the narrator's affect-less telling of the incident, which suggests to him "that neither Stephen nor Leopold aimed to feel much during that strange moment, that their respective defenses against tumult—Stephen repressing and intellectualizing, Bloom obsessing and digressing—served both of them well just then" (189).

Two further intriguing psychological justifications for Stephen's singing of the ballad curiously depend on turning Bloom into a perceived threat to Stephen and Stephen into a potential victim of Bloom's paternalism. Hugh Kenner comments that the story of *Ulysses* might have ended with Stephen's getting "everything he seemed to lack only that morning: decent quarters, a piano handy, a nubile woman about the place, the prospect of the nubile woman's daughter, time for literary pursuits, an indulgent provident 'father':

everything save freedom."[22] Kenner adds, "Bloom poses a real danger," and, "[b]earing the danger in mind, we can understand why Stephen sings the ballad about the imperiled Christian boy in the Jew's habitation, and departs within minutes of singing it" (139). But the timing of events in the episode does not logically support this argument. There has been absolutely no discussion prior to the singing of the ballad of Stephen's moving into the Bloom home, nor any conversation that suggests that such an offer is imminent. Bloom's offer, incredibly, comes immediately *after* Stephen's singing of the ballad, *not* before. While Vicki Mahaffey makes a similar argument—that Stephen perceives Bloom as a threat—she circumvents the issue of the timing of the offer by presenting a much fuller and more psychologically intricate and textured explanation of what she calls Stephen's "fearful prejudices"[23] against both Jews and women: "Stephen, in apparent contrast [to Bloom, who mourns a lost wholeness], perceives himself as having preserved his wholeness, and he holds onto his mental and emotional virginity with fierce integrity. He fears fragmentation, directing his fear at women and Jews, as those he believes most likely to disintegrate or symbolically castrate him" (260). Mahaffey's analysis has the virtue of fully detailing and acknowledging the virulence of the ballad and its singing,[24] but it too grounds its motivation in Stephen's fear of Bloom as a threat.

It is difficult to conceive of a better explanation for Stephen's singing of the song than that devised by Kenner and Mahaffey, but the justification resonates troublingly with Stephen's own interpretation of the ballad. By blaming the Christian boy and not the Jewish woman, Stephen makes the victim responsible for his own murder. For Kenner, and even more forcefully for Mahaffey, however, Stephen's perception of Bloom as a threat is spurious, a young man's delusion, and they do not directly fault Bloom for inciting Stephen's prejudicial fear. Nonetheless, although the aggression is undeserved, Bloom is designated as its trigger and cause. If Stephen's song is interpreted as a performative act in this respect, as designed to provoke a consequence and to repel Bloom from encroaching on Stephen's freedom or threatening his wholeness, then perhaps the text's sabotaging of the episode's climax has a similar performative function. By obliging the reader to

22. Hugh Kenner, *Ulysses*, rev. ed. (Baltimore: Johns Hopkins University Press, 1987), p. 139. Further references will be cited parenthetically in the text.

23. Vicki Mahaffey, "Sidereal Writing: Male Refractions and Malefactions in 'Ithaca,'" in *"Ulysses" En-Gendered Perspectives*, ed. Kimberly J. Devlin and Marilyn Reizbaum (Columbia: University of South Carolina Press, 1999), p. 262. Further references will be cited parenthetically in the text.

24. Mahaffey offers a highly detailed and deeply researched discussion of the provenance of the ballad and its variants (261-63), and she pays particular attention to its gender implications.

speculate on Stephen's motives in a way that will exonerate him by designating Bloom as a spurious threat, the text entrains the reader in the logic of anti-Semitism itself by presenting a potent temptation to blame the victim. The blood libel of the ballad of "Little Harry Hughes" is designed precisely to blame the victim, to justify the persecution of the Jews by positing them as a threat to the Christian community. The charge is groundless, "a pretense for plundering Jewish neighborhoods or expelling Jews from the country (such stories figured in the expulsion of Jews from Spain under Ferdinand and Isabella)," as Mahaffey argues (262) on the basis of the annotations to the ballad in Sir Francis Child's *The English and Scottish Popular Ballads*. If the reader is prompted to regard Bloom as both the spurious threat and the victim of Stephen's anti-Semitic attack, then we are not only made to serve witness to this tortuous and pernicious logic but to participate in an analysis of its construction. To understand why Stephen might wish to injure or offend Bloom with his ballad requires the reader to work through the logic of understanding how civilized peoples might persecute a minority by perceiving it, wrongly, as a threat. Bloom, of course, already possesses much understanding of this topic. He can tick off "the incitations of the hierarchy, the superstition of the populace, the propagation of rumour in continued fraction of veridicity, the envy of opulence, the influence of retaliation" (*U* 17.844-47) as explanations for "why the myth of ritual murder exists at all" (Davison 234). But for the reader during the era of *Ulysses*' writing and publication,[25] when anti-Semitism was rife even among intellectuals, a hermeneutical exercise more rigorous than merely hearing Bloom's explanation might seem required. Blood libel was by no means a thing of the past. Marilyn Reizbaum notes, "An incidence of blood libel, memorialized by Bernard Malamud in *The Fixer* (1959), occurred in Kiev in 1911, where a Jewish peasant was accused of murdering a Christian boy for such ritual purposes. The case was the subject of discussion all over Europe, including Ireland; many believed that this was a ritual practice of Jews everywhere" (13). The reader of the 1920s might still need to be forced to confront the temptation to exonerate Stephen by blaming his Jewish victim and to firmly resist that very temptation in the interest of justice.

---

25. Nadel, *Joyce and the Jews*; Davison, *James Joyce*; and Marilyn Reizbaum, *James Joyce's Judaic Other* (Stanford: Stanford University Press, 1999) all offer valuable historical context for Joyce's address to Jewish matters in *Ulysses*. Nadel cites the 1904 anti-Semitic attacks published by Arthur Griffith's *United Irishman*, with which Joyce would in all likelihood have been familiar. He also details the wide-ranging publicity generated by the Dreyfus affair and its consequences in the Irish and the Continental press (59-69). Further references to Reizbaum will be cited parenthetically in the text.

If Stephen's ballad was intended to force Bloom to retreat from a threatened intimacy, as Kenner and Mahaffey suggest, it fails and produces, inexplicably, the opposite effect. The conversation that follows Stephen's commentary on the ballad, if it is indeed delivered to Bloom, consists of Bloom's invitation to Stephen to remain and spend the night at his home. Why does Bloom bear no animus toward Stephen for his offensive gesture? The reader is once again obliged to speculate, and the best answer is probably that the ballad, prompting Bloom to think at some length with troubled affection about his daughter Milly, stirs his paternal feelings sufficiently to overcome any sense of offense. There is another possible explanation, however, that requires us to return to the ballad Stephen sang to Bloom as they began their journey to Eccles Street: the Johannes Jeep song about sirens who lure sailors to their death. Could Stephen, tired and muddled, with that earlier song still in his head, have selected "Little Harry Hughes" without malice, as an unthinking variant on the theme of the siren that surfaced previously in the Jeep ballad?[26] Might he then have been startled to recognize in Bloom's vanished smile after the second part that he has blundered and has caused a despicable, if inadvert, hurt? If so, his commentary turning little Harry into a masochistic martyr might be seen as a clumsy effort to save face, to mitigate the ballad's anti-Semitism in an effort to restore the geniality that the ballad has momentarily destroyed. Such an explanation assumes that the narrator's redaction of Stephen's commentary suppresses, in its allegorical abstraction, important components of the communication, particularly evidence of surprise, embarrassment, regret, and conciliatory desire on the part of Stephen. Lubomír Doležel notes that "today we know that the significance of nonverbal communication cannot be underestimated. A minor gesture or posture is often the sign of a great mental agitation" (99). Had Stephen evinced such a gesture or posture and Bloom registered it sufficiently to understand its meaning, then another small drama could be thought to have transpired behind the sabotaged climax without being registered by the narration. This last possibility is important because it offers a glimmer of hope that Stephen could yet play an important role in averting a disastrous future for Bloom. On this day when the ruin of Bloom's public reputation as a greedy, stingy Jew has been set in motion in Barney Kiernan's

---

26. Here is the reference to Stephen's singing of the Jeep ballad in "Eumaeus": "Even more he liked an old German song by Johannes Jeep about the clear sea and the voices of sirens, sweet murderers of men, which boggled Bloom a bit" (*U* 16.1812-14). Gifford and Seidman translate these lines as "From the Sirens' craftiness/ Poets make poems" (562). The text's reference to sirens as "sweet murderers of men" could prefigure the Jew's daughter in the ballad of "Little Harry Hughes" calling "*Come back, come back, you pretty little boy, / And play your ball again*" before she takes him to the room where she decapitates him (*U* 17.815).

pub, Bloom needs a friend and defender more than he knows. What if the malicious Alf Bergan tells the erroneous version of the Gold cup story to Stephen's father, Simon Dedalus, the next time he sees him, and the garrulous elder Dedalus begins to bruit it about Dublin? A Stephen at last alerted to Bloom's racial vulnerability could save Bloom from social devastation by countering the stereotype with his first-hand evidence of Bloom's generosity and kindness. Why would Joyce wish to obscure the possibility that Stephen's rudeness in singing the ballad might have been inadvertent? Perhaps because any explicit *excuse* for Stephen's behavior would simultaneously *absolve* the reader from concern about the ballad's anti-Semitism and its possible harm.

The conclusion that Stephen and Bloom fail to achieve paternal or familial communion in "Ithaca" has a long history, one that Richard M. Kain recapitulates in his essay, "The Significance of Stephen's Meeting Bloom: A Survey of Interpretations." Called "the Isolation Theory," since it posits the continued isolation of both Bloom and Stephen, this reading contends that their "meeting points up a tragic abyss between two temperaments, representative of the modern cultural crisis."[27] But the kind of rigorous tracking that contemporary narrative theory enables allows us not only to give this temperamental abyss between the novel's protagonists greater cultural specificity, it further provides a much sharper focus on its ethical and social stakes. These stakes could be as high as Leopold Bloom's social survival in Dublin, his ability to cling to the social margins he now inhabits rather than find himself inexplicably outcast altogether. As we have seen in "Cyclops," Bloom vigorously defends himself against anti-Semitism, when he is able to confront it. But if it is invisible and inaudible to him, he requires an active social intervention by someone on his behalf. Stephen appears poised as the only figure capable of playing that role. But the stakes may be even higher than this suggests. At the critical moment between Bloom's offer to Stephen to spend the night and Stephen's refusal, Bloom asks Stephen if he knew Mrs. Sinico, whose funeral Bloom attended the previous October. Stephen apparently did not. But in another instance of disnarration, we are told that Bloom suppresses an explanation with much greater relevance to Stephen, namely, that he missed Stephen's mother's funeral because he was away to observe the anniversary of his father's death. Why is Bloom specifically directed to think about these three deaths and funerals in the interval before Stephen responds to his offer? Here again the reader is prodded to speculate, and, at its most extreme, our speculation may suggest that it is not only Bloom's reputation that Stephen could save with his

27. Richard M. Kain, "The Significance of Stephen's Meeting Bloom: A Survey of Interpretations," in *"Ulysses": Fifty Years*, ed. Thomas F. Staley (Bloomington: Indiana University Press, 1974), p. 147.

friendship but perhaps even his life. The image of Mrs. Sinico's end, popping inexplicably into Bloom's mind between the time of his offer to Stephen and Stephen's refusal, along with the reminder of his father's death, may suggest that the threat of suicide also hangs over Bloom.[28] If the earlier trajectory of Bloom's increasing isolation continues and is intensified, the specter of ending life completely alone and in despair, like Emily Sinico and Rudolph Bloom, will perhaps loom before him if Molly ever leaves him or dies.

Instead of offering the long awaited convergence of Stephen and Bloom at the end of the novel, the text confounds and confuses any satisfactory resolution to the relationship. This interpretive dilemma has been produced by Joyce's complex narrative strategy in "Ithaca," one that deploys a seemingly authoritative voice to withhold information, confuse fact and supposition, and thereby incite painful questions without offering adequate resources to draw reasonable inferences and satisfying conclusions. Resort to narrative theory offers conceptual clarification about the conditions of narratorial authority that can impose limits on possibilities of authentication, while pointing to the stakes of narrative language that functions performatively not only in the relations among the characters but in relation to the reader as well.[29] The ballad of "Little Harry Hughes" not only *means* something, as it is performed by Stephen in Bloom's kitchen, it also *does* something to Bloom and, by implication, to Stephen. In the process, it also *does* something to the reader. The reader is pointedly notified that alertness to the operation and effects of anti-Semitism are critically important if Stephen is to serve as Bloom's friend and possible savior. The same alertness is demanded of the reader. Joyce's acute anatomy of anti-Semitism in *Ulysses*

28. David Wright, "The Secret Life of Leopold Bloom and Emily Sinico," *JJQ* 37.1/2 (Fall 1999/Winter 2000): pp. 99-112, has speculated at length about this curious and putatively "inconsequent" intrusion of Mrs. Sinico into one of the last reported conversations between Bloom and Stephen in the novel. Although Bloom seems to describe her as "accidentally killed" (*U* 17.945-47) in his question to Stephen, Wright suggests that Bloom speculates about her lonely and possibly suicidal end. "So we are bound to ask: does Bloom's concern with the details of Emily Sinico's death, and his apparent association of her with his own father (who seems to have killed himself partly because of loneliness), suggest that he knew enough about her to wonder whether she had taken her life deliberately and, moreover, to imagine why she might have done so?" (108).

29. Narratologists have for some time been concerned with breaking the constraints that the field's theoretical apparatus might pose to its hopes of transcending a narrow formalism. Mieke Bal, in *Narratology: Introduction to the Theory of Narrative*, 2nd ed. (Toronto: University of Toronto Press, 1997), addresses this issue both in her Introduction and in her Afterword, and J. Hillis Miller, in *The Ethics of Reading* (New York: Columbia Univ. Press, 1987), makes the even more forceful point that "ethics itself has a peculiar relation to that form of language we call narrative" (3).

not only impels the reader passively to register its representation, it also requires the reader actively to sort out its operation and thereby play an ethical role in its intervention. This may be why Joyce defrauds the reader of a sentimental climax, of a utopian satisfaction in seeing Bloom rewarded for his goodness by having a son restored to him and seeing Stephen's intellectual integrity at last warmed by the nurturing embrace of a humane father. By shocking the reader with Stephen's anti-Semitic ballad at the climax of the novel, Joyce forces us to explore why such outbursts are produced, to reexamine their historical origins, and to worry about their pernicious future effects not only on Leopold Bloom, but more widely on an entire European population.

University of California, Irvine

THE SHAKESPEAREAN DEMIURGE IN JOYCE'S FORGE[1]

STEPHEN WHITTAKER

Abstract: Near the centers of *Ulysses* and *Finnegans Wake*
Joyce models the forge of artistic creation as an abstraction of
the female pelvis, an image originating in Plato's *Timaeus*
wherein divine, artistic, and sexual making are isomorphic. In
the *Wake* Shem tricks Shaun into drawing a figure from Euclid
that also depicts their mother's reproductive and excretory
organs. Stephen's aesthetic theory in *Ulysses* unfolds amidst
comparable imagery. Although Plato and Homer are its
generative elements, both renderings of Joyce's forge cast
Shakespeare as the Demiurge, the agent of creation in Plato.

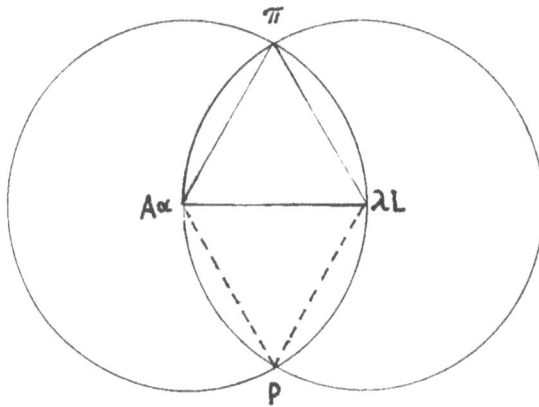

Near the centers of *Ulysses* and *Finnegans Wake* Joyce constructs elaborate
expositions on the nature of creation. In *Ulysses* chapter nine Stephen offers
his Shakespeare theory. Between thinking of Mulligan's "First he tickled her/
Then he patted her/ Then he passed the female catheter" (*U* 9.22-24) and
encountering Bloom fresh from inspecting the posterior of a statue of Venus,
Stephen sketches a picture of artistic making in which the creator's creation
recapitulates his ontogeny. In *Finnegans Wake* chapter X Shem tricks Shaun
into drawing the geometric figure that begins Euclid's *Elements*, a figure that

---

1. This essay is part of a larger manuscript, titled "Joyce's Forge: Plato, Homer,
Shakespeare, and the Smithy of the Soul."

also apparently depicts their mother's pelvis. Textual details further identify the design as that laid out in Plato's *Timaeus* for the cosmic forge wherein all creation comes into being. Although explicit at the center of the *Wake*, this geometric figure occurs more subtly, but no less certainly or significantly, at the center of *Ulysses*. Both central depictions of the forge include the figure of the demiurge, the agent of creation in the system of *Timaeus*, and in both Joyce casts Shakespeare in the role.

The Forge of *Timaeus* in *Finnegans Wake*

Ellmann recounts a conversation between Joyce and Jacques Mercanton that occurred as Joyce neared completion of the *Wake*. According to Ellmann, Joyce, who compared writing the *Wake* to the activity of the demiurge, "was explaining the plan of a section" of the *Wake* "when he suddenly paused to ask" a rhetorical question that Ellmann renders from Joyce's French as, "Isn't this the way the demiurge must calculate in making our fine world?" Ellmann continues to translate Joyce's remarks: "I reconstruct the life of the night the way the demiurge goes about his creation, on the basis of a mental scenario that never varies. The only difference is that I obey laws that I have not chosen. And he?" (*JJII* 707-8). In *A Skeleton Key to Finnegans Wake* Campbell and Robinson note that in the first half of chapter X of the *Wake*, "twenty-six pages (260-86) are devoted to the description of the descent of spirit into time and space."[2] The demiurge functions in *Timaeus* to effect this descent of logos into chaos to create cosmos. Clive Hart observes that in the *Wake* Joyce "shows a general knowledge of Plato"[3] and uses *Timaeus* comprehensively.

In *Structure and Motif in Finnegans Wake* Hart argues that Joyce derived both the spatial cycles and the cosmic chiasmus motif of the *Wake* from Plato's *Timaeus* and that "the description in *Timaeus*," which Joyce's text embodies, "of the creation of the World-Soul, if not the archetype of this particular mystic symbol in western literature, is at least one of the most important early appearances" (129). Of the crossing of Shem and Shaun in the Geometry Lesson in *Wake* II.2, or, appropriately, chapter X, Hart writes: "That in disposing his materials in this way Joyce had *Timaeus* in mind is made clear by the inclusion of a whole shower of allusions to it. At 288.03, in particular" (132). And further:

2. Joseph Campbell and Henry Morton Robinson, *A Skeleton Key to "Finnegans Wake"* (New York: Viking, 1967), p. 163. Further references will be cited parenthetically in the text.
3. Clive Hart, *Structure and Motif in "Finnegans Wake"* (Evanston: Northeastern University Press, 1962), p. 150. Further references will be cited parenthetically in the text.

78

> Joyce makes undistorted use of the terminology of the *Timaeus* at 300.20, where Shem and Shaun are called the 'Other' and the 'Same' respectively, while the 'Other', as in Plato, is made to move to the left 'with his sinister Cyclopes'. These are the 'twinnt Platonic yearlings' (292.30) whose mutual rotation is described as 'spirals' wobbles pursuiting their rovinghamilton selves'. (Hart 133)

Though he is certain that Joyce uses Plato throughout the *Wake*, Hart opines that Joyce came "to *Timaeus* through *A Vision*," an idea refuted by the presence of *Timaeus* in *Ulysses* fifteen years before Yeats' *A Vision*. Hart concludes that, "whatever his direct source may have been," Joyce "used the theories for all he was worth" (129). Recent critics such as Brivic, McCarthy, and Solomon accept Hart's identification of the Platonic source of these structural details.[4]

Three features of *Timaeus* are of ubiquitous importance to *Finnegans Wake*: the nature of creation, the structure of created things, and the isomorphism of all creations. The first, the nature of creation, links the realms of logos and eros. In creation logos descends into chaos to form cosmos. As Joyce reads *Timaeus*, chaos—contained in the receptacle, the womb of creation—lures logos' fall. Rather than *ex nihilo*, in the act of creation a logos or order is imposed upon an existent material chaos, the elements of which, though disordered, are characterized by necessity. The structure of this transformation of chaos into cosmos is a double X formed by the intersections of two cosmic circles at an angle to each other. The word *chaosmos* (*FW* 118.21) in the *Wake* enacts this imposition upon chaos of cosmos in the form of an X, or a chiasmus.

As Brion observed in "The Idea of Time in the Work of James Joyce" in *Our exagmination*, in words recalling exactly *Timaeus'* picture of creation, *Work in Progress* seeks to convey "a reality true and whole in itself" which will "obey its own laws and appear to be liberated from the customary physical restraints."[5] This obedience to an intrinsic logos distinguishes Platonic views of creation from Aristotelian. Aristotle's art object imitates the laws of the external world; Plato's, like that world, generates and adheres to its own internal rules. That the *materials* of the Platonic art object must of

---

4. Sheldon Brivic, *Joyce the Creator* (Madison: University of Wisconsin Press, 1985), p. 121. Patrick A. McCarthy, *The Riddles of "Finnegans Wake"* (Rutherford: Fairleigh Dickinson University Press, 1980), p. 99; and Margaret Solomon, *Eternal Geomater: The Sexual Universe of "Finnegans Wake"* (Carbondale: Southern Illinois University Press, 1969), p. 108.
5. Marcel Brion, "The Idea of Time in the Work of James Joyce," in *Our Exagmination Round His Factification for Incamination of Work in Progress* (New York: New Directions Books, 1962), p. 33.

course follow the rules of the real world is their necessity. In transforming language in the *Wake*, Joyce must use the necessities of language. *Chaosmos* reflects the rules of construction for the *Wake* and does so in terms of the restrictions of its constituent wide-awake English words. Joyce does not create a new language *ex nihilo*; he imposes new order on pre-existing fragments. Like the *T, tea, thea*, which, Campbell and Robinson note, pervades the *Wake,* the logos stains the previously existent water of creation (163n2). Joyce's remarks to Mercanton concern internally versus externally generated laws.

For Atherton the *Wake* embraces the heresy that the creation and fall are one.[6] The young ALP, in the form of Issy, tempts the creator, until the "maker mates with made, (O my!)" (*FW* 261.08). Though above Earwicker, she is heard from below, thanks to the acoustics of their chimneys, as Gordon notes.[7] Brivic says she is the "ondrawer of our unconscionable."[8] In *Timaeus* the logos, through the demiurge, contemplates its own form and reproduces itself through creation. Jowett's 1892 gloss on *Timaeus* summarizes the dynamic of creation: "And so the thought of God made a God in the image of a perfect body, having intercourse with himself and needing no other, but in every part harmonious and self-contained and truly blessed."[9] Thus creation is a form of self-seduction or onanism, a theme replete in the *Wake*. In this context Joyce explicitly compares his activity in writing the *Wake* with the activity of the demiurge.

The second feature of *Timaeus* permeating the *Wake* is the fact that all created things, from Grace O'Malley's riddle to the river's end, are triangles, deltas. We will return to this.

Third, along with the concept of the demiurge, *Timaeus* introduced the concept of the isomorphism of microcosm and macrocosm. All small creations—creatures—resemble larger ones. As Bishop shows,[10] the fallen giant whose "*feats end enormous, your volumes immense*" (*FW* 419.5) is the individual body, the city, its environs, even Europe and the heavens. This equation of all scales of world-body occurs in the signature at the head of

6. James Atherton, *The Books at the Wake: A Study of Literary Allusions in James Joyce's "Finnegans Wake"* (Carbondale: Southern Illinois University Press, 1974), pp. 30-31.

7. John Gordon, *"Finnegans Wake": A Plot Summary* (Syracuse: University of Syracuse Press, 1986), p. 12. Further references will be cited parenthetically in the text.

8. Sheldon Brivic, "The Mind Factory: Kabbalah in *Finnegans Wake*," *James Joyce Quarterly* 21.1 (Fall 1983): p. 17, quoted in Gordon, *"Finnegans Wake,"* p. 186.

9. Benjamin Jowett, trans., *Dialogues of Plato*, vol. 3. (Oxford: Clarendon Press, 1892; Bristol: Thoemmes Press, 1997), p. 354.

10. John Bishop, *Joyce's Book of the Dark* (Madison: University of Wisconsin Press, 1986), pp. 35-37.

Stephen's *Book of Elements* in *Portrait* (*P* 15) and is suggested in the link traced between HCE the dreamer and *hoc est corpus* of the Mass. The central doctrine of the god/cosmos who has become an individual body allowed Saint Augustine and many other Christian theologians to suppose Plato prescient of the Trinitarian mystery.

HCE's immense volume is also the volume *Finnegans Wake*—the book/universe of "Doublends Jined" (*FW* 20.16)—which in its circularity is a single turn, a uni-verse. As the *Skeleton Key* has it, "Maya's memorial to the absolute is the cosmos; ALP's memorial to HCE is her letter" (Campbell and Robinson 97n1). *Timaeus* uniquely links the idea of creation as the remembering (re-membering) of logos with the micro/macro equation by which ALP's letter and the universe and the body and the book remember each other. The reader, like the logos, is lured to impose some logic at "the beginning of all thisorder" (*FW* 540.19), and to "(Stoop) if you are abcedminded, to this claybook" (*FW* 18.17). *Timaeus* treats reading the *Wake* as well as writing it. Both activities are creation, the descent of logos into that which seems a chaos but which has its own necessities. Brivic writes that "The interface of the double-aspect text resides in the area where the mechanical figures in the text meld with the psychic being that generates them."[11] At the interface of the circle of the same and the circle of the other in *Timaeus*, God, mind, or logos looks down into world, body, or eros, and the creature likewise gazes upward at its creator. This reversibility of perspective is mirrored everywhere in the *Wake*, in such phrases as the dazzling "whom will comes over" (*FW* 260.4) early in chapter X.

In the *Wake*—a book, body, world, cosmos, mind—the made make. We are "finight mens mid infinite true" (*FW* 505.24-25): finite night mind mid infinite logos, the paradigmatic logon, where sexual, physical and divine creations converge in, as Gordon says, "a multi-layered chronicle reviewing private and universal history culminating in a moment of sexual, generative, and eucharistic transformation."[12] Creation in *Timaeus* and the *Wake* merges thought thinking thought with a sex act at once conjugal, onanistic, and incestuous: "Behose our handmades for the lured!" (*FW* 239.10).

Where the *Elements*' figure is two dimensional, that in *Timaeus* is three. *Timaeus* describes two cosmic circles, one within the other, a wheel of sameness and a wheel of difference. The wheels turn on a common center, and their two points of intersection describe two great X's, or *chi's*, which persist though the points on the wheels which generate them move. In cross grinding the two intersecting wheels of this mill allow the descent of logos to their central chaos, imposing thereupon a new cosmos; as in the word *chaosmos,* in cosmogenesis the crossing or chiasmus brings cosmos out of

11. Brivic, *Joyce the Creator*, p. 59.
12. Gordon, *"Finnegans Wake,"* p. 183.

chaos.

The *Wake* abounds with names for the forge which emphasize both its geometry and the sexual, artistic, and cosmic realms of creation. Some names emphasize Plato and Euclid: "chaosmos" (*FW* 118.21), "youthlit's bike" (*FW* 270. 23), "the zeroic couplet" (*FW* 284.10), and "the Platonic garlens" (*FW* 623.36). Some stress geometry: "crisscrossed Greek ees" (*FW* 120.19), "our twain of doubling bicirculars" (FW 295.30-31), and "the hardest crux ever" (*FW* 623.33-34). Some emphasize sex: "bisexcycle" (*FW* 115.16), "eroscope" (*FW* 431.14), and the elaborate "Concaving now convexly to the semidemihemispheres and, from the female angle" (*FW* 508.21-22). Some echo conceptual structure; "chaosmos" is followed by mention of "the continually more and less intermisunderstanding minds of the anticollaborators" (*FW* 118.24-26) and "our home homoplate" (*FW* 119.03). The question, "then *what* would that fargazer seem to seemself to seem seeming of, dimm it all?" (*FW* 143.26-27), yields, "A collideorscape" (*FW*143.28). Conceptual structure likewise emerges in "mirrorminded curiositease" (*FW* 576.24). Some names emphasize the equation of the body of ALP, the text of the *Wake*, and the world: "this radiooscillating epiepistle" (*FW* 108.24), "me elementator joyclid" (*FW* 302.12), "ann aquilittoral dryankle Probe loom" (*FW* 286.19-20), "an equoangular trilliter" (*FW* 286.21-22), "Plutonic loveliaks twinnt Platonic yearlings" (*FW* 292.30-31), and, most famously, "the whome of your eternal geomater." (*FW* 296.31-297.1).

The Forge Before the Wake

Chiastic structures abound in Joyce; they are part of the metaphysics, which is to say aesthetics, of his creation. Bloom seeks an ad comprised of crossed keys in a circle. The model of creation in *Timaeus* saturates the villanelle section of *Portrait*. The poem and prose narrative, in counterpoint, interweave sexual, artistic, and divine creation; Stephen creates the villanelle even as he is being created, and both the episode and the poem are conspicuously circular and chiastic. "The Sisters" similarly inscribes this figure: the narrator as creature circles twice between the priest's house and his own; he traverses the ground of the story twice, once as character/creature, again as creator/narrator.

The first paragraph of "The Sisters" mentions the gnomon, from the start of Euclid's *Elements*, Book II. If one takes a small parallelogram from one corner of a larger proportional parallelogram, a gnomon remains. The word means "that by which something may be known," and it occurs in the story as one of three italicized words which encapsulate the Platonic metaphysics of Joyce's creation, wherein broken perceptions both bar understanding and make it possible to move past them to understanding. The words—

"*paralysis*," "*gnomon*," and "*simony*" (*D* 9)—anatomize this doubling of concealment and revelation in the realms of body, world, and God. *Paralysis* cleaves body and mind, *gnomon* the defective thing and its absent form, and *simony* the earthly and divine. Together they point beyond their specific provinces to a general metaphysical property manifest throughout the story and exemplified by the opening image of the creator as creature studying a screen that both conceals the Father and affords clues by which dialectic might reveal his presence. Though it is thus a gnomon, when the boy sees that screen he imagines a different geometrical figure. He imagines two candles by a corpse and supposes their reflections on the blind. The result would be not the *gnomon*'s lazy L, but two overlapping circles of light, the figure in the middle of the *Wake*, where it represents in geometry the womb of cosmogenesis and effects thereby the synthesis of three italicized words that begin Joyce's *oeuvre*. This figure, the first in Euclid's *Elements*, is the method of constructing an equilateral triangle. One figure from Euclid conceals another, which, like Blake and Yeats, conceals Plato. An emblem of how the work comes into being, the intersecting circles appear throughout Joyce, always, until the *Wake*, covertly.

The figure in *Timaeus* does not reference Euclid. Euclid followed Plato by a century and was educated in his academy. Rather, Euclid, like Joyce, opens with this figure as a reference to *Timaeus*, which describes the creation of deltas, whether divine creation of the cosmos, any human making (poesis) in the world, or sexual reproduction. The figure emblematizes the manner of connectedness of the three realms of Joyce's italicized words. So when Shem leads Shaun to draw the figure, Shem thereby supplies part of the *Wake*, delivers on his promise to reveal how the world is made, and tricks his stodgy brother into sketching their mother's external organs of generation.

Timaeus says that the circles create by means of an intermediary, a demiurge. They create the demiurge and instruct it to create the cosmos in the same manner as it, the demiurge, was created. The created world has the form of triangles. In Joyce's creations triangles center the circles and their chiasmuses. For example, "A Boarding House" features the two spheres of Mrs. and Polly Mooney. Each is a phase of the other. The one, the arc of the old moon, begins the narrative, and ends her section gazing toward her daughter, and into a mirror. The other, the arc of the new moon, ends the narrative and her section gazing toward her mother, and into a mirror. Between the mirroring women, Bob Doran falls into the new world they have made for him. As he walks down the stairs he passes Polly's brother, who carries two bottles of Bass Ale. The label on each features a triangle within a circle. Jack carries two triangles within two circles past the descending Bob. Narrative form and content mimic the forge.

Triangles likewise emerge at the center of "The Sisters" and at the end of "The Dead." When the image of the bisexcycle in the *Wake*, referenced as a stereopticon, is so viewed, the image resolves into a single circle with six radii, each equiangular from the next. This image is referenced at the center of the various pairs of circles that comprise "The Sisters." The narrator remembers a sign that hung in the window of the shop beneath Fr. Flynn's on ordinary days and which offered to re-cover the spokes of an umbrella. This detail in Joyce's frontispiece story links several Platonic themes important to *Timaeus*. Etymologically, "Umbrellas Re-covered" suggests the reincarnation of souls in the process of birth. In fact, the sign is covered in the story and exists only as a memory prompted by its own absence. This detail reminds us further that, although Shem will lead Shaun to draw the forge of sexual, artistic, and cosmic genesis from *Timaeus*, the original story in Plato of one character leading another to draw a triangle occurs in *Meno*. In that dialogue Socrates leads Meno's uneducated servant to derive the Pythagorean theorem, and thence concludes that all knowledge of the world arrives via memory from before our birth, thereby equating geometry (the measure of the created world), sexual creation, and the deepest mysteries of the cosmos. The stereoscopically consolidated circle of the forge, with its six spokes, appears throughout the *Wake* in references which identify the cosmos of the *Wake* as an umbrella: "penumbrella" (*FW* 462.21), "old preadamite with his two handled umbrella" (*FW* 530.28-29), and "umbrilla-parasoul" (*FW* 569.20). The complex nature of the cosmic umbrella as a thing which reveals by concealing can be seen in phrases such as "expending umniverse" (*FW* 410.17), "Annexing then ... concealed a concealer" (*FW* 484.10-14), and "the unaveiling memory of" (*FW* 503.26-27).

Similarly, at the end of "The Dead" Joyce constructs the image of the forge as triangles of creation fall through the center of that most celebrated double chiasmus:

> It was falling on every part of the dark central plain, on the treeless hills, *falling softly* upon the Bog of Allen and, farther westward, *softly falling* into the dark mutinous Shannon waves. It was falling, too, upon every part of the lonely churchyard on the hill where Michael Furey lay buried. It lay thickly drifted on the *crooked crosses* and headstones, on the spears of the little gate, on the barren thorns. His soul swooned slowly as he heard the snow *falling faintly* through the universe and *faintly falling*, like the descent of their last end, upon all the living and the dead. (*D* 223-4; my emphasis)

Gabriel imagines a churchyard of crooked crosses, X's, and considers the transition between the worlds of the living and the dead. He watches "the flakes, silver and dark, falling obliquely against the lamplight." The flakes fall through a chiasmus of words and through the universe onto all of creation, each flake a unique six-spoked precipitate of solid matter out of cloud.

In a letter to Grant Richards in 1906 Joyce wrote of *Dubliners*, "I have written my book with considerable care, in spite of a hundred difficulties and in accordance with what I understand to be the classical tradition of my art" (*Letters I* 60). Although his claim of working in a classical tradition may have struck Richards as posturing, Joyce in fact composed the stories according to an aesthetic modeled in Plato.

Shakespeare as Demiurge and Bloom as Shakespeare in *Ulysses*

Two scenes argue Shakespeare's function as demiurge in Joyce. Curiously, although the geometry of the forge is subtle in *Ulysses*, the identity of the demiurge is clear, while, by contrast, although the geometry of the forge is explicit in the *Wake*, the identity of the demiurge appears only in a glitter of etymologies.

Forty-four lines after the forge at the center of the *Wake*, before "the whome of your eternal geomater" (*FW* 296.31-297.1), occur these three sentences: "And for a night of thoughtsendyures and a day. As Great Shapesphere puns it. In effect, I remumble, from the yules gone by, purr lil murrerof myhind, so she used indeed" (*FW* 295.3-6). McHugh finds three references in sentence one: "*The Thousand Nights & a Night (Arabian Nights)*," "II Peter 3:8: 'one day is with the Lord as a thousand years,'" and "night of 1,000 years in 'The Historical Cones', diagram in Yeats' *A Vision* 266." He says of sentence two, "Shakespeare" and "A Vision 187: 'ultimate reality, symbolized as the Sphere'." He says of three, "remember," "years (Xmases)," "mirror," "little Mother of Mine," "behind," and "mind."[13] Sentence one links Scheherazade's stories to Christian and Platonic cosmogonies. Three juggles themes common to Plato's *Meno* and *Timaeus*: the linking of knowledge, memory, and birth, both human and divine. To understand two requires a more careful look at it and one. With respect to one, Campbell and Robinson find, "The sister heroines of the *Arabian Thousand Nights and One Night*, who regaled King Shahryar with their endless story cycle, and thus distracted him from his cruel design to ravish and slay a maid a night. They are comparable to the Two Temptresses in the Park. Their bedside tales correspond to ALP's letter and *Finnegans Wake* itself" (57n2). Thus sentence one links the theological, geometrical, and artistic realms of the *Wake*.

Sentence two links one and three via etymology. Skeat traces "shape" to

---

13. Roland McHugh, *Annotations to "Finnegans Wake*," 3d ed. (Baltimore: Johns Hopkins University Press, 2006), p. 295.

roots meaning *to form, to make,* and *to create.*[14] "Shapesphere" creates a globe: the world and its best-known stage. The sphere is great, as in the great circles of a globe, but also its shaper is great, and great with offspring. For "pun," Skeat finds, "to pound, to beat; hence to *pun* is to pound words, to beat them into new senses."[15] In *Ulysses* chapter three, between *Nacheinander* and *Nebeneinander*, Stephen walks on breaking shells "made by the mallet of Los *demiurgos*" (*U* 3.17-18). Stephen thinks of Blake's demiurge, Los, hammering the world into being. Like Los, Shakespeare pounds the world, the realm of poesis, and the body of the mother, all globes, into being. McHugh *et alia* understandably mistake Yeats as the source of the Platonic material in the *Wake*; the text promotes the error. Stephen finds his source for the demiurge not in Plato, but in an intermediate, Blake. Joyce points us not to Plato but to his descendants; such intermediation is the way of demiurges.

Stephen's Shakespeare talk in the national library in *Ulysses* chapter nine occurs within Homeric and Platonic paradigms. Joyce's schematae for *Ulysses* give Homer's *Odyssey* as a key structuring device. Stephen's talk mediates Homer's Scylla and Charybdis. *Timaeus'* forge of creation structures Joyce's work from the beginning and affords the model of how the elements of *The Odyssey* participate, which suggests the comparable preliminary nature of his dialogues. Stephen's talk occurs between Eglinton's "Upon my word it makes my blood boil to hear anyone compare Aristotle with Plato" (*U* 9.80-81) and the suggestion that Stephen recast his theory as a Platonic dialogue, arguably what Joyce has done in *Ulysses* chapter nine. Joyce calls his book *Ulysses* a translation of Odysseus. Richard Klonoski has shown that the first re-performance, that is, translation, of Homer's Odysseus was Plato's Socrates.[16]

"Two left" (*U* 9.15), Stephen thinks as "Scylla and Charybdis" opens. Socrates begins *Timaeus* likewise: "One, two, three: but where, my dear Timaeus, is the fourth ... ?"[17] Socrates addresses Critias, poet and orator, and Timaeus, a compendium of all learning, Jowett says.[18] Stephen addresses the oracular Russell and Eglinton, the librarian (*U* 9.46). *Timaeus* tells how intersecting circles of sameness and difference, the latter in seven parts,

14. W.W. Skeat, *An Etymological Dictionary of the English Language*, 1st ed. (Oxford: Clarendon Press, 1882), p. 545.

15. Skeat, *Etymological Dictionary*, p. 477.

16. Richard J. Klonoski, "The Preservation of Homeric Tradition: Heroic Re-Performance in *The Republic* and *The Odyssey*," *Clio* 22.3 (1993): p. 271.

17. Plato, *Timaeus*, in *The Dialogues of Plato*, vol. 3, trans. Benjamin Jowett (Oxford: Clarendon Press, 1892; Bristol: Thoemmes Press, 1997), p. 437. Further references will be cited parenthetically in the text.

18. Jowett, *Dialogues of Plato*, p. 345.

structure Cosmos (455). Charybdis, from the depths below, threatens to swallow everything. Scylla, the seven-headed monster above, threatens to divide and slaughter Odysseus' men. Plato accounts for the fact that we can understand the world via the application of dialectic, the mental processes of synthesis (sameness) and analysis (difference). Scylla and Charybdis writ large are the cosmic forces of difference and sameness. Stephen offers his theory within overlapping Homeric and Platonic paradigms: Homer's Charybdis versus Scylla; Plato's ideal unity versus material multiplicity. But when he is challenged to discuss how creation works, Stephen resorts overtly to neither of the scene's key texts, but rather to Shakespeare, whom he shows creating in the manner of his own making, out of the materials of his own life. *Timaeus* says demiurges make, in the manner of their own making, the three mortal kinds remaining to be generated: the inhabitants of air, water and earth, the realms of simony, paralysis, and gnomon.

Shakespeare appears more conspicuously in Joyce's fiction than does any other poet. In *Ulysses* chapter nine, challenged on how creations come into being, Stephen turns to Shakespeare. Stephen's *Hamlet* theory, burlesqued eight episodes earlier by Mulligan, argues that Shakespeare rendered the shape of his own life in his plays, participated in his own creations as creature, and modeled his artistic offspring on his deceased son. Buck foretold that Shakespeare, or is it Stephen (Haines is unsure), is his own grandfather. Stephen's Shakespeare, like Plato's demiurge, makes as he himself was made.

That the Shakespearean paradigm for his own creation is itself based on the Homeric and Platonic paradigmata is, in "Scylla and Charybdis," lost on Stephen, but certainly not on Joyce, who has brought Stephen's world into being with Shakespeare its demiurge. As Schwaber observes, Stephen's theory fulfills its own description of what Shakespeare did in the plays; both have "fathered verbally crafted dramatis personae who were transformations" of themselves.[19] Stephen argues in effect that Shakespeare is made potent by his own sexual subordination by Ann Hathaway. The demiurge creates out of its being a creature. It is drawn to creation by contemplation of its own uncreated self; its chaos and necessity lure its own idea into re-creation. As does Stephen's Shakespeare, Joyce fashions his artistic creation according to his own coming into being. The action of *Ulysses* chapter nine springs in part from Joyce's sense of usurpation and betrayal, by a supposed friend who would displace him, and by a publisher who will tempt him to sell his art. *Ulysses* chapter nine appeals to Shakespeare on theoretical grounds and makes use of him as demiurge. Stephen says, as Joyce might, "—His own image to a man with that queer thing genius is the standard of all experience,

19. Paul Schwaber, *The Cast of Characters: A Reading of "Ulysses"* (New Haven: Yale University Press, 1999), p. 36.

material and moral" (*U* 9.432-35).

Unwittingly playing a nice variation on Stephen's Hamlet theory, Eglinton quotes enthusiastically, "After God Shakespeare has created most" (*U* 9.1028-29). Eglinton then bobbles the attribution: "When all is said Dumas *fils* (or is it Dumas *père*?) is right" (*U* 9.1028). Don Gifford notes it was the *père* who was accounting for his own becoming a playwright.[20] The quotation puts Shakespeare in the demiurge's relation to God, and the citation emphasizes that the elder Dumas was brought into being as a creator by the example of Shakespeare, a greater shaper. Thus, Dumas' *père* becomes an artistic *père* by being *fils* to Shakespeare's creations, and, like the demiurge, is a *père* because he is a *fils*, and vice versa. But Eglinton protests Stephen's theory: "You have brought us all this way to show us a French triangle. Do you believe your own theory?" (*U* 9.1064-65). If we understand "French triangle" a little more broadly than Gifford's "The relationship among the three people involved in an adultery; man-wife-lover, etc.,"[21] we can see that Eglinton is right; Stephen has shown us the creative triangle of sexual, as well as artistic, creation. Eglinton, like Shaun in the *Wake*, feels tricked. He cannot see the aptness of Shakespeare's performing the role of a generative triangle at the heart of this chapter. Best, however, tells Stephen, who has just declared disbelief in his own theory (*U* 9.1065), that he "ought to make it a dialogue, don't you know, like the Platonic dialogues Wilde wrote" (9.1068-69). Joyce will do something like this in *Ulysses* chapter nine. Stephen immediately begins the process of making the scene, in the globe of his own head: "One day in the National Library we had a discussion. Shakes" (*U* 9.1108).

That Shakespeare is both the son and father of *Ulysses* chapter nine appears most sublimely through the identification of Shakespeare and Bloom. Half a century ago, William Schutte identified Bloom with the cuckolded Shakespeare created in Stephen's narration.[22] More recent studies have reaffirmed and extended Schutte's argument.[23] Parallels abound. For

20. Don Gifford with Robert J. Seidman, *"Ulysses" Annotated: Notes for James Joyce's "Ulysses,"* rev. ed. (Berkeley: University of California Press, 1988), p. 249.

21. Gifford and Seidman, *"Ulysses" Annotated*, p. 251.

22. William M. Schutte, *Joyce and Shakespeare: A Study in the Meaning of "Ulysses,"* Yale Studies in English 134 (New Haven: Yale University Press, 1957).

23. Richard Halpern, *Shakespeare Among the Moderns* (Cornell: Cornell University Press, 1997), p. 168. Also, Ira Nadel, *Joyce and the Jews* (Iowa: University of Iowa Press, 1989); Neil R. Davison, *James Joyce, "Ulysses," and the Construction of Jewish Identity: Culture, Biography, and 'the Jew' in Modernist Europe* (Cambridge: Cambridge University Press, 1998); Lois Feuer, "Joyce the Postmodern: Shakespeare as Character in *Ulysses*," in *The Author as Character*, ed. Ton Hoenselaars and Paul Franssen (New Jersey: Fairleigh Dickinson University Press, 1999); Gary Goldstein, "Who Was Joyce's Shakespeare?," *Elizabethan Review* 5.1 (1997): pp. 26-31; and

example, when Stephen wonders, regarding Shakespeare, "And why no other children born? And his first child a girl?" (*U* 9.1135), the connection to Bloom, and the parallel between Hamnet and Rudy, is unavoidable, as is the further link of Burbage and Hamlet, as surrogates for Shakespeare, to Stephen's comparable function for Bloom. The peculiar link between Stephen and Bloom, via Shakespeare, appears graphically in *Ulysses* chapter fifteen, where "Stephen and Bloom gaze in the mirror. The face of William Shakespeare, beardless, appears there, rigid in facial paralysis, crowned by the reflection of the reindeer antlered hatrack in the hall" (*U* 15.3821-22).

Just as Stephen's disquisition upon the Shakespearean corpus occurs conceptually within Platonic and Homeric contexts in chapter nine, so it occurs, dramatically, within Leopold Bloom's double quest. At the end of chapter eight, before Stephen begins his talk in chapter nine, Bloom panics at the unexpected sight of Boylan. Bloom thinks, "Look for something I" (*U* 8.1182), and he dives into the library and its "cream curves of stone" (*U* 8.1180). Bloom has come on business. Hoping to sell ad space for the House of Keyes, and having failed to conjure its design verbally, he has come to find a copy of an earlier printing in the library's newspaper files. When Bloom describes the ad, it is the image of the forge: "Like that, see. Two Crossed Keys here. A circle" (*U* 7.142). As *Timaeus* puts it:

> This entire compound he divided lengthways into two parts, which he joined to one another at the centre like the letter X, and bent them into a circular form, connecting them with themselves and each other at the point opposite to their original meeting-point; and, comprehending them in a uniform revolution upon the same axis, he made the one the outer and the other the inner circle. (454)

But Bloom is on a second quest. When he and Stephen pass one another at the end of chapter nine, after Stephen has completed his Shakespeare theory, Bloom has just attempted inspection of the beautiful buttocks of the statue of Venus for their anatomical accuracy. He searches art for the biology of the divine, searches creation for the body of God, and searches the gnomon for the paralysis of simony. Bloom, about whom there is a touch of the artist, brings a layman's enthusiasm to a consideration of what, in the *Wake*, will be described as "Concaving now convexly to the semidemihemispheres and, from the female angle" (*FW* 508.21). At the posterior of chapter nine, at what may be understood to be the exact center of *Ulysses*, Bloom has sought for the very image that Shem will elicit illicitly from Shaun at the center of the *Wake*. Just as the crossed keys are within a single circle, we can see, like the

Matthew Creasy, "Shakespeare Burlesque in *Ulysses*," *Essays in Criticism: A Quarterly Journal of Literary Criticism* 55.2 (2005): pp. 136-58.

consolidated image of a stereopticon, what Bloom cannot: that Bloom's two quest objects are one, the forge. Bloom has dived into his quest for the two forms of the forge, driven, like Shakespeare, by a French triangle.

The French triangle of Stephen's Shakespearean demiurge in "Scylla and Charybdis" nests within Bloom's double quest for the figure of the forge: one in the divine female body of art, the other in the geometry of a punning advertisement. The divine female artwork links cosmos, bios, and poesis, as well as their problematics (simony, paralysis, and gnomon). The crossed keys and the statuary pelvis converge in Stephen's theory. As the great Shapesphere punned it, "There's a divinity that shapes our ends, Rough-hew them how we will."[24]

On 16 June 1904 Stephen trembles within the most profound revelation of his creative life: the structure of the forge, where Shakespeare functions as demiurge of creation inside the overarching Platonic and Homeric paradigms, and wherein the creature becomes creator in the manner of his creation. Joyce contextualizes Stephen's Shakespearean aesthetic within Bloom's quest for his also not quite synthesized manifestations of the forge. By the time he writes *Ulysses* Joyce has long since worked out the structure of the forge. Before *Ulysses* he concealed the image of the forge repeatedly, strikingly even in *Dubliners*. In work he will start within days of the date of Bloom's and Stephen's encounter, Joyce, creator, *père* and *fils*, will begin a story which will come to have the form of the forge; a story in which creature and creator, boy and narrator, are the same yet different; a story which resembles uncannily that which structures Stephen theory; a ghost story which reshapes the experiences of a Dublin youth in the borrowed vestments of a vanished Dane; a story about a boy, of an age with Hamnet, who lives, like Hamlet, in this Uncle's house; a story which opens with this fatherless youth watching alone, night after night, for some sign of the fate of the Father. That Father will appear, in a dream perchance, and attempt to confess, as though he had died with his sins upon him, and the story will end with a corpse, an empty chalice, and silence. "The Sisters" marks the birth of the Joyce we know and, though Stephen may not quite see it, 16 June 1904 memorializes the occasion of James Joyce's key epiphany concerning the nature of creation.

University of Scranton, Pennsylvania

24. William Shakespeare, *Hamlet* 5.2.10.

PLAYING THE SQUARE CIRCLE: MUSICAL FORM AND POLYPHONY IN THE *WAKE*

ALAN SHOCKLEY

Abstract: Several times in his letters, Joyce refers to *Finnegans Wake* as a work of music, and he describes his writing of it as a musical activity. In addition to hundreds of allusions to opera and popular song in the novel's text, both the micro and macro structures of the *Wake* can be viewed as musical in nature. Using tiny excerpts from a Bach fugue and the *Wake* as examples of similar polyphonies, this essay shows how the circularity and contrapuntal nature of the *Wake* call on readers to approach Joyce's last novel, not as a literary object, but as a musical performance.

> *Finnegans Wake . . . is first of all an Irish-American song of drink and resurrection.*[1]

To tackle even a small part of *Finnegans Wake*, this colossal "legpull," is a mammoth task. People with broader and deeper knowledge of opera and of popular song than I have begun the Herculean job of cataloguing Joyce's musical allusions within the *Wake*. I agree with Mabel Worthington: "Sometimes I have the sense that every word in *Finnegans Wake* is a musical allusion."[2] *Finnegans Wake* is a novel that doesn't work like a novel. Anthony Burgess, while writing about *Dubliners*, espies the problem for all of Joyce's prose works: "The stories in *Dubliners* are different . . . [from those of other writers]: nothing seems to happen in them, there are no plots, they are not really stories at all."[3] So, too, *Finnegans Wake*: it contains no recognizable action, and if it has a plot, it is so simplistic that most writers would eschew using it even to underpin a short story, much less to bolster a large novel.

So the lists, lexicons, censuses, plot summaries, and "skeleton keys" written for the *Wake* explicate very little substance—this novel rests on so little. An Irish-American popular song, "Finnegan's Wake" (also known as

1. Ruth H. Bauerle, ed., *Picking Up Airs: Hearing the Music in Joyce's Text* (Urbana: University of Illinois Press, 1993), p. 3.

2. Mabel Worthington, quoted in Bauerle, *Picking Up Airs*, p. 1.

3. Anthony Burgess, *Here Comes Everybody: An introduction to James Joyce for the Ordinary Reader* (London: Faber and Faber, 1965), p. 19. Further references will be cited parenthetically in the text.

"The Ballad of Tim Finnegan"), provides the title for Joyce's work, and also the novel's paltry story: Tim Finnegan, a hod carrier (or bricklayer), is a bit of a drinker. One morning Finnegan slips on a ladder and breaks his skull. His friends lay out the body and throw him a lively wake. But the wake quickly devolves into a brawl and bottles fly. One gallon of whiskey (the Gaelic "water of life") misses its intended target and falls on Finnegan, who revives and shows surprise that his friends believe him deceased.

Here we have the fundamental pun of the novel: Finnegan's *wake*, his funeral gathering, is also his awakening, his resurrection. This story doesn't provide an ending; rather, it inscribes a circle. Or, as the *Wake* puts it, "[I]t was mutualiter foretold of him by a timekiller to his spacemaker, velos ambos and arubyat knychts, with their tales within wheels and stucks between spokes, on the hike from Elmstree to Stene and back" (*FW* 247.1-5).

As in *Ulysses*, Joyce wants to free his novel from the chafing constraints of time: "Of course the unskilled singer continues to pervert our wiser ears by subordinating the space-element, that is to sing, the *aria*, to the time-factor, which ought to be killed, *ill tempor*" (164.32-35).[4] Time should not only be made subservient to space, it "ought to be killed." Again, Anthony Burgess describes the Joycean dilemma: "Time remains the enemy; history must be spatialised. How? By seeing it as a circle, a wheel perpetually turning, the same events recurring again and again" (191). So on one level, *Finnegans Wake* inscribes the circle of the song, the story of Tim Finnegan: a rise, a fall, another rising and the implication that this pattern repeats itself endlessly. But the star of this show is not the titular character, but another incarnation of him and his circular story: Humphrey Chimpden Earwicker.

The same circularity of Tim Finnegan's fall and "resurrection" speaks from the Earwicker family story. Shem and Shaun seem to be two halves of their father, as well as the male heir(s) set to supplant him. Issy is a young version of her mother, and Earwicker seems to have an incestuous attachment to her. Earwicker has had a fall, though not a literal one. He has committed a sin, has embarrassed himself and his family in some way. This nameless sin may be that he has exposed himself in Phoenix Park. He also may have played the peeping Tom to a couple of young girls urinating behind some bushes. This dreamscape presents little with clarity, so the two young girls seem to be Earwicker's own daughter, replicated mirror-fashion, just as her brothers reflect each other (and just as each son presents half of the image of his father).

4. *Il tempo* means "the time." *Illo tempore* means "at that time" and is a recurring phrase beginning gospel readings. Roland McHugh, *Annotations to "Finnegans Wake*," rev. ed. (Baltimore and London: The Johns Hopkins University Press, 1991), p. 164.

Harry Burrell argues that the *Ur*-story for the *Wake* is Biblical, and that a short section of the book of Genesis provides the *only* story present in the *Wake*: "the third chapter of Genesis, reinterpreted and repeated hundreds of times, is the narrative base of *Finnegans Wake*. All of the events are simply reenactments of the Fall story. There is no action which does not contain Adam and Eve's travail in the Garden of Eden."[5] Most critics, whether or not they accept the Genesis story as the sole tale of Joyce's novel, see its simple plot and cast of characters replicated in many different ways.

I will consider several ideas concerning the music of and in the *Wake*, beginning with a brief exploration of the novel's circular form and the musical implications of this circularity. Next, by drawing an analogy to Bach's polyphony, I offer my own "key" to *Finnegans Wake*, a method not for explaining and labeling each reference, but, I hope, for providing a satisfactory reading of the novel.

The Circular Novel

As in *Ulysses*, in *Finnegans Wake* Joyce looked outside the novel tradition for forms and chooses, this time, a shape from a theory of human history: Vico's *Scienza Nuova* and its circular view of history. Vico divided human history into three ages and a section preparing for a repetition of the cycle: the ages of gods, heroes, men, and the *ricorso*. A thunderclap sets the wheel of history into motion, and its three ages may be represented within the human life cycle as birth, marriage, and burial, followed by a pause before resurrection (the ricorso).[6] So, too, Joyce divides his novel into four books.[7] On a smaller scale the books are further subdivided into chapters, and these

5. Harry Burrell, *Narrative Design in "Finnegans Wake": The "Wake" Lock Picked* (Gainesville: University Press of Florida, 1996), p. 7. Many critics find only a single story for the *Wake*, some look only at heraldry in the novel, at children's lore, or at Irish pre-Christian rites, and one traces only the novel's references to Sherlock Holmes. See chapter V of Michael J. O'Shea's *James Joyce and Heraldry* (Albany: State University of New York Press, 1986), Grace Eckley's *Children's Lore in "Finnegans Wake"* (Syracuse, N.Y.: Syracuse University Press, 1985), George Cinclair Gibson's *Wake Rites: The Ancient Irish Rituals of "Finnegans Wake"* (Gainesville: University Press of Florida, 2005), and William D. Jenkins' *The Adventure of the Detected Detective: Sherlock Holmes in James Joyce's "Finnegans Wake"* (Westport, C.T.: Greenwood Press, 1998).

6. See the sample encyclopedia entry on Giambattista Vico in McHugh, *Annotations*, p. xi.

7. Joyce also uses the thunderclap; *Finnegans Wake* contains ten "thunderwords," the first one of which appears on the first page of the text: "[B]ababadalgharaghtaka-mminarronnkonnbronntonnerronntuonnthunntrovarrhounawanskawntoohoohoordenen thurnuk!" (*FW* 3.15-16).

too reflect Joyce's interpretation of the Viconian cycle (see Example 1).[8]
Wheels within wheels. Joyce's symbol for the form of this novel is a square
wheel: "No, it's a wheel, I tell the world. *And* it's all *square*."[9] The larger
wheel divides into four quadrants, and these too participate in circularity.
Telescoping in to the surface level of the form, *Finnegans Wake* begins not
with a beginning but *in medias res*, as in the beginning of many myths, and
enacts this form at the level of the sentence: "riverrun, past Eve and Adam's,
from swerve of shore to bend of bay, brings us by a commodius vicus of
recirculation back to Howth Castle and Environs" (*FW* 3.1-3). This
sentence's beginning ends the book with an incomplete phrase and an absent
end-stop: Joyce's "A way a lone a last a loved a long the" provides no
conclusion but an ending that is also *in medias res* (*FW* 628.15-16). As
Burgess explains: "That first sentence is the only one of the whole book that
begins without a capital letter. Joyce tells us why in the word 'vicus' (Latin
for Vico) and also in 'recirculation'. We are not beginning; we are resuming.
History is a circle as Vico taught, and we have entered it in the middle of a
sentence. ... Time may have a stop but history's wheel is in perpetual
motion" (196-97). In a letter to Harriet Weaver, Joyce jokingly describes his
intention: "The book really has no beginning or end. (Trade secret, registered
at Stationers Hall) It ends in the middle of a sentence and begins in the
middle of the same sentence."[10] Circularity was central to Joyce's vision of
the *Wake* from its conception.

The Musicality of a Circular Form

Repetition and recurrence, which define musical forms, contradict the form
of the novel. Joyce's choice of circles within circles not only points to Vico,
but also gives at least a nod toward the writing of *Finnegans Wake* as a
musical text. Circular forms are common in music. For example, in the rondo
form listed in Example 2, the "A" is a theme or a section that keeps
returning—and a rondo could theoretically continue forever. As Richard
Ellmann recounts of Joyce explaining his work on *Ulysses*: "Writing a novel,
... [Joyce] said, was like composing music, with the same elements
involved" (*JJII* 436). Years later Joyce referred to *Finnegans Wake* in similar
terms: "The musical aspect of the book was one of its justifications. 'Lord

8. Many commentators—beginning within Joyce's circle with Samuel Beckett—
have researched the use of Vico in the *Wake*; a brief and perceptive discussion of the
specific appeal of the *Principi di Scienza Nuova* to Joyce appears in Umberto Eco's
The Aesthetics of Chaosmos: The Middle Ages of James Joyce, trans. Ellen Esrock
(Cambridge: Harvard University Press, 1989), pp. 62-70.
9. James Joyce to Harriet Shaw Weaver (postcard), 16 April 1927 (*SL* 321).
10. James Joyce to Harriet Shaw Weaver, 8 November 1926 (*SL* 314).

knows what my prose means,' he [Joyce] wrote his daughter. 'In a word, it is pleasing to the ear. . . . That is enough, it seems to me'" (*JJII* 702).

Musical Analyses of the *Wake*

With the *Wake*, as with the "Sirens" episode of *Ulysses*, Joyce again pointed critics toward musical form and techniques, referring to the novel as his "'suite' in the key of E-flat,"[11] and calling the "Anna Livia Plurabelle" chapter "his 'melodic' chapter."[12] Ruth Bauerle suggests why Joyce's last novel refers to music so much: "Joyce's dependence upon music increased as his blindness forced him more and more into an oral/aural world. It is partly for this reason that *Finnegans Wake* includes more music than all the other works combined."[13] A few critics have scoured the *Wake* for musical references (as Matthew Hodgart and Ruth Bauerle do in *Joyce's Grand Operoar*,[14] finding all the references to *Don Giovanni*, for instance); a few analysts have even searched the novel's letters for encoded music. But reading the *Wake* as musical code has its pitfalls—it's far too easy to find musical clues everywhere.

The *Wake*'s Musical Development; the Novelist's "Required" Musical Performance

The density of language of *Finnegans Wake* has led some readers to declare that it's not written in English at all, and they may have a point—so many words of the novel are compounds of some sort, each syllable participating in multiple "lines" of thought and imagery, and often in multiple languages as well.[15] This text seems to require that its reading be like a performance of a contrapuntal musical piece.

11. As quoted in Jack W. Weaver, *Joyce's Music and Noise: Theme and Variation in His Writings* (Gainesville: University Press of Florida, 1998), p. 4.
12. Edna O'Brien, *James Joyce* (New York: Viking Penguin, 1999), p. 141.
13. Bauerle, *Picking Up Airs*, p. 3. Eric McLuhan gives an alternate, yet equally convincing explanation for the aural nature of the *Wake*: "It is noteworthy that we do not have earlids as we have eyelids. That is, even during sleep, our ears are as active as they are during the day, whereas our outward vision is shut down. Bearing in mind that *FW* is a 'night book,' the ears might be found to be particularly active." Eric McLuhan, *The Role of Thunder in "Finnegans Wake"* (Toronto: University of Toronto Press, 1997), p. 311n8.
14. Matthew J.C. Hodgart and Ruth Bauerle, *Joyce's Grand Operoar* (Urbana: University of Illinois Press, 1997).
15. Michael Frayn labeled this novel's language "Eurish," or Euro-Irish-English, and Anthony Burgess, Christopher Prendergast, John Cowan, and others have adopted this apt term.

I think this is part of the point. Joyce wrote and rewrote *Finnegans Wake*, packing additional references into each new version of a passage, increasing the density to such a point that no single reader (other than Joyce himself) could address the many references of a single paragraph or page, much less a chapter, or the novel as a whole. Explanations, annotations, less formal "musings" on selections from the novel appeared almost as soon as the first excerpt found its way to publication. Joyce eventually admitted to giving such projects as *His Exagmination Round His Factification for Work in Progress* much more than encouragement.[16] He practically commissioned such explications. The result is a text that cannot be read like any other. Joyce made it almost impossible to start with the first word of the first page and continue reading left-to-right without pause to the last word of page 628. Nonetheless, I think such a reading is exactly what this text requires. Since the text makes it impossible to catch all or even most of the references it makes, since a large proportion of the cultural baggage it carries has a Joycean stamp on it that obscures some of its meaning from all but the author, the reader is forced to surrender to the momentum of the text. A good reader of this text, like a good listener of a densely polyphonic piece from the Baroque period, must hop on at the beginning of the ride and hang on for dear life until the last of it. To continue my analogy, both works (the *Wake* and an exemplar of Baroque polyphony) are motoric: both repeat and develop simple themes in complex ways and in multiple, simultaneous layers. Both works exist in time and yet work to defeat time through the constant recurrence of thematic and sub-thematic material. Both works require multiple "readings" if they are to disclose their significant structural workings.

So, in a contrapuntal work from the Baroque period, in, say, the restricted texture of a three-voice fugue by Bach, every note participates in many different lines of the music. A note may last only a fraction of a second, and its meaning for the piece as a whole may be only partially uncovered in a single listening experience; in fact, its full meaning may remain uncertain even after repeated listening. Let's look at a single note in a short excerpt from Bach's Fugue XVI in G minor from the *Well-Tempered Clavier*, Book I (see Example 3).[17]

---

16. In a letter to Valéry Larbaud, Joyce writes that he oversaw "those twelve Marshals more or less directing them what lines of research to follow." James Joyce letter to Valéry Larbaud, 30 July 1929 (quoted in *JJII* 613). The "twelve Marshals" made *Exagmination* like Earwicker's bar with its twelve customers, or Christ's twelve (*JJII* 613).

17. Johann Sebastian Bach, *Das Wohltemperierte Klavier*, ed. Otto von Irmer (Munich: G. Henle Verlag, 1974), p. 81. All references to the fugue refer to this edition.

The circled note, an F-sharp, participates in many different motivic and linear trajectories for this piece. In the overall key of the piece this F-sharp is the leading tone (or scale-degree 7), and, as such, it has some standard grammatical functions in the tonal language of Bach, much as a word in the English language has set functions in Shakespeare's writings. In a horizontal succession the F-sharp follows a D, an E-flat, and a G in the tenor part and is in turn followed by another G. In like manner, as a verticality, this F-sharp literally sounds simultaneously with C in the bass and A, C, and E-flat in the upper parts, forming a full harmony. F-sharp acts as a lower neighbor note to the tenor G's that precede and follow it. F-sharp is part of the "local" dominant here, and it needs to resolve to G, an expectation left partially unfulfilled for a few more beats. (As both a neighbor and as a note of the local dominant, F-sharp stands in for G, keeping G ever present—in a listener's expectations at least.) This F-sharp harmony is connected by function and shared pitches with harmonies reaching back to at least measure 28 of the piece. F-sharp is also the fourth note in this fugue's eleven-note subject—which means that it's thematically related to every other occurrence of the subject (for example, measure one to measure two in the alto part, measures 28-29 in the soprano, etc.) and also to every other note of the entire fugue since this is a single subject fugue, and, essentially, a monothematic composition (see Example 4).

Something similar occurs with words in *Finnegans Wake*:

> And this is why any simple philadolphus of a fool you like to dress, an athemisthued lowtownian, exlegged phatrisight, may be awfully green to one side of him and fruitfully blue on the other which will not screen him however from appealing to my gropesarching eyes, through the strongholes of my acropoll, as a boosted blasted bleating blatant bloaten blasphorus blesphorous idiot who kennot tail a bomb from a *painapple* when he steals one and wannot psing his psalmen with the cong in our gregational pompoms with the canting crew. (*FW* 167.8-17; emphasis mine)

The word "painapple" connects through simple adjacency and left-to-right English language conventions with the entire rest of this lengthy sentence, but it's proximally most connected with the words "a" and "when." It's part of a prepositional phrase, "from a painapple." And, as part of this prepositional phrase, it forms a consequent to the antecedent construction "who kennot tail a bomb." Painapple is close enough in spelling and sound to the familiar "pineapple" that the reader immediately thinks of this word also and accepts the neologism as a noun functioning in this prepositional phrase, perhaps as a substitute for "pineapple." Standing in for "pineapple" makes that word present here as well, though the "correct" name for the fruit does not appear in this passage or near it. Just as F-sharp keeps G present even while literally displacing G in a lower neighbor figure in the Bach example, so "painapple" both displaces and keeps "pineapple" here for the reader.)

"Pain" and forms of the word "pine" can both be traced to a single parent word, first through *peine* (affliction, sorrow, punishment) and eventually to the Vulgar Latin *pena*, meaning "penalty" or "punishment." So Joyce's neologism connects pain or sorrow and pineapple. Placing the word "bomb" so close to "painapple" in the line also refers to a slang use of the word "pineapple": it's a nickname for a hand grenade, which, like bombs, causes pain and death.

The fall of man, especially the idea of the fortunate fall, is everywhere in *Finnegans Wake*. As mentioned earlier, Harry Burrell has proposed that this novel contains no other story at all, that every page of the *Wake* retells the same story from Genesis. Whether or not we accept such economy of means for each page of the novel, the Biblical story is certainly at work here: taking of the fruit of the Tree of Knowledge of Good and Evil is mankind's first sin, and eating it brings punishment. It also brings pain and sorrow, for, as Genesis 3:16 explains, "Unto the woman ... [God] said, 'I will greatly multiply thy sorrow and thy conception; in sorrow thou shalt bring forth children." God continues to Adam, "Because thou hast hearkened unto the voice of thy wife, and hast eaten of the tree ... cursed [is] the ground for thy sake; in sorrow shalt thou eat [of] it all the days of thy life."[18] At the end of the Genesis passage, God determines that humankind cannot be trusted to remain in the Garden, and so imposes the ultimate pain—the pain of death—upon them and banishes Adam and Eve from Eden.[19] Eating of the fruit in the Garden leads to pain. Joyce's ambiguous fruit (is it a pain- and punishment-causing apple? is it a pineapple?) recalls the Genesis references: the type of fruit is never mentioned in the Bible, though tradition, along with Dante and Milton, deems it to have been an apple.[20]

18. Genesis 3:16-17, *King James Bible*.
19. In Sheridan's *The Rivals*, one of Mrs. Malaprop's many verbal blunders is to use "pineapple" when she intends "pinnacle": "Sir—you overpower me with good-breeding. He is the very pineapple of politeness!" Perhaps Joyce is also connecting Eden's fruit with Sheridan's. This particular pineapple (and, hence "painapple") brings Eve and Adam to their anti-pinnacle, their nadir. Richard Brinsley Sheridan, *The Rivals*, ed. Elizabeth Duthie (London: Ernest Benn Limited, 1979), p. 62.
20. Perhaps there's another, related reason for the choice of pineapple for the fruit here: pineapple has, since America's Colonial period, been a symbol of welcome and of hospitality. The fruit in the Genesis story leads to banishment. So, a "painapple" is a symbol of anti-welcome. I've already mentioned the unnamed fruit of Genesis; in Milton's *Paradise Lost*, Eve names the alluring fruit: "To satisfy the sharp desire I had / Of tasting those fair apples, I resolv'd / Not to defer" (9.584-86).

Just as F-sharp connects with other notes throughout the Bach fugue, this word also resonates with words on other pages of the novel. This "painapple" on page 167 speaks across pages, echoing and being echoed elsewhere:

> or these are not on terms, they twain, bartrossers, since their baffle of Whatalose when Adam Leftus and the devil took our hindmost, gegifting her with his painapple, nor will not be atoned at all in fight to no finish, that dark deed doer, this wellwilled wooer, Jerkoff and Eatsoup, Yem or Yan, while felixed is who culpas does and harm's worth healing and Brune is bad French for Jour d'Anno. (*FW* 246.26-32)

Neither of these *Wake* passages is transparent in a single reading, but "O felix culpa" ("O fortunate fall!") appears in this second passage in the phrase "felixed is who culpas does," recalling Augustine's understanding of the incident in the Garden as necessary to bring about God's sending a second Adam. Christ's death and resurrection balance Adam's fall—or, more profanely, Tim Finnegan's fall from a ladder balances his rise (seemingly from death) at the touch of whiskey. So, this "painapple" returns us to the Fall of Adam and Eve, but it also repeats the story of Tim Finnegan, the myth of the phoenix, and all the other incarnations of the circular story that make up *Finnegans Wake*.

Though Joyce disliked both Jung and Freud, his treatment of individual words as vertices wherein hundreds of polyphonic lines may intersect seems related to a statement of Freud's: "A word, being a point of junction for a number of conceptions, possesses, so to speak, a predestined ambiguity."[21] Such complex webs of reference as the "painapple" one have led many critics to remark on the polyphony of *Finnegans Wake*. Examining one particularly dense section of the *Wake*, Burgess even drew the analogy between this prose and Bach's polyphony: "This part of *Finnegans Wake* is the very devil to summarise: it is like saying what Bach's *Art of the Fugue* is about, bar by bar" (230).

---

21. Sigmund Freud, *The Interpretation of Dreams*, trans. A. A. Brill, 3d ed. (London: Allen and Unwin, 1919), p. 315, quoted in James S. Atherton, *The Books at the Wake: A Study of Literary Allusions in James Joyce's "Finnegans Wake"* (New York: The Viking Press, 1960), p. 39. In summarizing the structure and the "structural books" of the *Wake*, Atherton gives, in outline form, a concise reading of the axioms of Joyce's novel (53). Within this, three statements draw connections from Freud back to Bruno: "As each atom has its own individual life (according to Bruno) so each letter in *Finnegans Wake* has its own individuality. . . . Each word tends to reflect in its own structure the structure of the *Wake*. (Bruno, the Cabbala.). . . . Each word has 'a predestined ambiguity' (Freud), and a natural tendency to slide into another state (Bruno)."

Yet the analogy breaks down beyond a certain point. The contrapuntal nature of much of *Finnegans Wake* crosses and recrosses cultural lines, literary styles, languages, epochs. Bach's polyphony in a fugue from the *W.T.C.* is German, and clearly of its time and its place. Bach's polyphony is ever constrained by harmonic considerations, while the *Wake* seems always poised to break free of all constraints, even those of the printed page. But the analogy remains a useful tool for approaching the dense text of the *Wake*, which most readers confronting the pages of Joyce's last novel need. As James Atherton remarks, "To read through the book once is a full-time occupation for a week, providing that the reader is prepared to continue reading without pausing to consider the meaning of the words before him. If he does stop to consider there is no limit to the time he may spend; indeed Joyce claimed that he expected his readers to devote their lives to his book."[22] I offer, instead, this musical experience of the *Wake*, drawing on a common way of experiencing contrapuntal music.

Finnegans Wake does not assert its musicality, but it does reveal musical preoccupations. It has a title and the caricature of a story borrowed from a popular song, and it is packed full of song lyrics and opera libretto references. Joyce takes from Vico a view of history that looks more like a dance form than any of the linear constructs offered by most historians (and novelists). His text isn't overtly musical, but it *is* a very musical text. Rather than developing a single cast of characters through the exigencies of a captivating plot, Joyce intensely develops recurring images and finds ways of echoing his cast across time, across cultures, against sense itself. To "kill the time element," Joyce activates the language of the *Wake* so that each sentence, each word, and even individual syllables participate in multiple lines of development. Through many layers of editing he created a densely polyphonic text, one that demands to be read in a fashion analogous to the way a listener approaches a polyphonic piece of music. Perhaps the *Wake* doesn't read like a piece by Bach, or any extant musical work, but it asks its readers to listen to its counterpoint, to join the dance at any point and to hold on breathlessly.

California State University, Long Beach

---

22. Atherton, *The Books at the Wake*, p. 11.

100

Example 1: Chart of the Viconian Cycle of the Novel

I. Divine Age	II. Heroic Age	III. Human Age	IV. *Ricorso*
1. Divine Age	9. Divine Age	13. Divine Age	17. Divine Age
2. Heroic Age	10. Heroic Age	14. Heroic Age	
3. Human Age	11. Human Age	15. Human Age	
4. *Ricorso*	12. *Ricorso*	16. *Ricorso*	
5. Divine Age			
6. Heroic Age			
7. Human Age			
8. *Ricorso*			

Example 2: Some Circular Musical Forms

Minuet or Scherzo form (An example of a compound ternary form.)

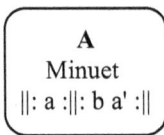

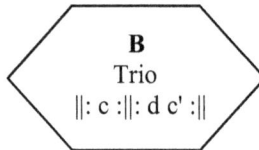

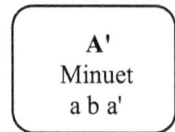

A
Minuet
||: a :||: b a' :||

B
Trio
||: c :||: d c' :||

A'
Minuet
a b a'

Rondo form

A B A' C A'' B A'''

Concerto Grosso (ritornello form)

tutti-solo-tutti-solo-tutti-solo-tutti, etc.
(The tutti sections are the ritornelli [the returns], and the final ritornello is exactly as the opening one—though the intermediary ones may be abbreviated or presented in different keys.)

Ternary form (includes the Baroque *da capo* aria, many marches, polkas, etc. Within the Baroque dance suite pairs of dances are often grouped into compound ternary forms, such as gavotte-bourée-gavotte.)

A B A'

Example 3: Fugue XVI, Measures 33-34

Example 4: Two Other Presentations of the Subject

Subject, mm. 12-13, alto

Subject, mm. 28-29, soprano

CONTRIBUTORS

Susan Adams is a PhD Economist who also happens to teach and research Joyce when the economists aren't looking. She was a student in Coilin Owens's *Finnegans Wake* seminar at George Mason University, where she was on the Economics faculty. Susan has taught at the Joyce Summer School in Dublin and has been a presenter/participant at various Joyce events around the world, including the Brisbane Joyce Summer Schools. Susan brought out the first Vietnamese translation of Joyce in 2005 while living in Hanoi, and has recently written a play about Joyce and Ho Chi Minh (who both lived in Paris in 1920), which will be produced in 2009 in Vietnam.

Austin Briggs, who was educated at Harvard and Columbia, retired as Hamilton B. Tompkins Professor of English Literature, Emeritus, from Hamilton College after teaching there for fifty years. He has also taught in Joyce summer programs in Dublin, Trieste, and Dubrovnik. The author of *The Novels of Harold Frederic*, he has published many essays on Joyce.

Alan W. Friedman is Thaman Professor of English and Comparative Literature at the University of Texas at Austin, specializing in twentieth-century British and American literature, while also regularly teaching Shakespeare. He has taught at universities in England, Ireland, and France. Among his six authored books are *Party Pieces: Oral Storytelling and Social Performance in Joyce and Beckett* (2007) and *Fictional Death and the Modernist Enterprise* (1995; reprinted 2008). His six edited books include *Beckett in Black and Red: The Translations for Nancy Cunard's Negro*. With Charles Rossman, he is currently co-editing three other special issues of journals on Joyce and Beckett.

Margot Norris is Chancellor's Professor of English and Comparative Literature at the University of California, Irvine, where she teaches twentieth-century literature and intellectual history. She is the author of six books, including *Beasts of the Modern Imagination: Darwin, Nietzsche, Kafka, Ernst and Lawrence* (1985) and *Writing War in the Twentieth Century* (2000). Her four books on James Joyce include *The Decentered Universe of "Finnegans Wake"* (1976), *Joyce's Web* (1992), *Suspicious Readings of Joyce's "Dubliners"* (2003), and a study of the Joseph Strick film of Joyce's *Ulysses* published in 2004. She is also the editor of the 2006 Norton Critical Edition of James Joyce's *Dubliners*. Between 2004 and 2008, she served as President of the International James Joyce Foundation.

Tara Prescott is completing a Ph.D. in twentieth-century American literature at Claremont Graduate University, working on a dissertation focusing on the poetry of Mina Loy. Her love of Joyce has been fueled by working with Colleen Jaurretche and Al Wachtel, as well as by the year she spent studying Joyce at the National University of Ireland, Galway. She currently teaches film and literature at the University of Redlands.

Charles Rossman is Professor of English and Distinguished University Teaching Professor at the University of Texas, Austin. He has published widely on James Joyce, D.H. Lawrence, and Latin American novelists of the so-called "Boom." His publications include two volumes, one each on Mario Vargas Llosa and Beckett, co-edited with Alan Friedman.

Alan Shockley holds the Ph.D. in music composition from Princeton University, and he composes for small and large ensembles, soloists, and electronics. He is an Assistant Professor of Composition/Theory at California State University, Long Beach. Of late, his research, on various musically structured modernist novels, has evolved from a paper about "Sirens" and many attempts at reading a fugue within *Ulysses*. His first book, *Music in the Words*, which grew out of this work and expanded to include not only Joyce, but also novels by Anthony Burgess, David Markson, William Gaddis, and others, is forthcoming from Ashgate Press.

Stephen Whittaker is Professor of English and teaches philosophy in the Special Jesuit Liberal Arts Program at the University of Scranton. He has published several articles on Joyce and is completing a book titled *Joyce's Forge: Plato, Homer, Shakespeare and the Smithy of the Soul.*

David G. Wright (1952-2008) was a Senior Lecturer in English at The University of Auckland, having previously taught at the University of Toronto and Victoria University of Wellington. His published books include *Characters of Joyce* (1983), *Yeats's Myth of Self* (1987), *Ironies of Ulysses* (1991), and *Joyita: Solving the Mystery* (2002). At the time of his death he had just completed a book on the relationship between the characters of *Dubliners* and *Ulysses* entitled *Dubliners and Ulysses: Bonds of Character.*

www.ingramcontent.com/pod-product-compliance
Lightning Source LLC
Chambersburg PA
CBHW050526280326
41932CB00014B/2471